EASTON COLLEGE
LEARNING RESOURCE CE

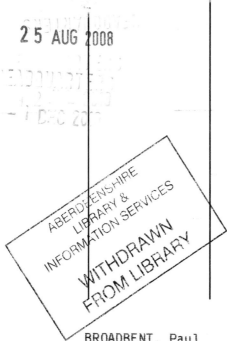
BROADBENT, Paul

Goalkeeper

Master the Game
Goalkeeper

Paul Broadbent and Andrew Allen

HODDER
EDUCATION
PART OF HACHETTE LIVRE UK

All photographs have been provided by Action Images Ltd.

Fitness Disclaimer

The information in this book is designed only to help you make informed decisions about health and fitness. It is not intended as any kind of substitute for the advice or treatment that may have been prescribed by your doctor.

Before following any of the information or recommendations in this book, you should get an assessment of your overall health from your doctor to ensure that it's safe for you to exercise.

You're solely responsible for the way you view and use the information in this book, and do so at your own risk. The authors are not responsible in any way for any kind of injuries or health problems that might occur due to using this book or following the advice in it.

Every effort has been made to trace the correct copyright holders of this work, but if any have been inadvertently overlooked the publisher will be pleased to make the necessary arrangements at the first opportunity.

Orders: please contact Bookpoint Ltd, 130 Milton Park, Abingdon, Oxon OX14 4SB. Telephone: (44) 01235 827720. Fax: (44) 01235 400454. Lines are open from 9.00–5.00, Monday to Saturday, with a 24-hour message answering service. You can also order through our website www.hoddereducation.co.uk.

British Library Cataloguing in Publication Data
A catalogue record for this title is available from the British Library.

ISBN-13: 978 034092 8400

First Published   2008
Impression number   10 9 8 7 6 5 4 3 2 1
Year   2012 2011 2010 2009 2008

Typeset by Servis Filmsetting Ltd, Manchester.
Printed in Great Britain for Hodder Education, part of Hachette Livre UK,
338 Euston Road, London NW1 3BH by Cox and Wyman Ltd, Reading, Berkshire.

Contents

Introduction

Football is without doubt the most popular sport in the world. In a recent survey carried out by FIFA (Fédération Internationale de Football Association), the world football governing body, it was estimated that there are 265 million male and female players worldwide. A pleasing sign in this survey is the continuing growth of the women's game. Over recent years girls' football in particular has seen a massive growth in popularity and has now become the fastest growing sport for girls.

For many young people, football is played in order to 'live the dream' of becoming a professional player. This only becomes a reality for a small percentage, so in most cases the appeal of the game is largely social and for pure enjoyment, with the added health benefit of increased fitness. Whatever the reason, all young footballers aspire to play at their highest level and full potential. It is not uncommon for a keen young footballer to go through their early playing career without the regular support of a qualified football coach. These players, however, are still keen to improve their skills and develop their game.

This book has been written to support players to reach their full potential, allowing all young footballers to develop their game, either on their own or with their friends. Following the practices and drills within the book, reading the top tips and testing themselves at the end of each chapter, will give young players the opportunity to increase their knowledge and develop their game.

It is widely accepted that the more you practise, the better your game will become. This applies to football just as much as it does to any other sport. Knowing the correct techniques, understanding and applying tactical elements and analysing team play will allow young players to develop their game and improve their chances of success.

This book is one of a series of four books covering four key positions within the modern game: Goalkeeper, Defender, Midfielder and Striker. Each book contains tips, drills, practices and techniques applicable to the respective positions. There are also chapters within each book that will be of general interest to all footballers, relating to fitness, diet, equipment and dealing with injuries, as well as advice on finding the right club.

Football can certainly be 'a beautiful game' as Pelé once famously stated. With careful physical and mental preparation, increased understanding of the game and relevant practice of skills and techniques, you can play your part in this wonderful sport. We hope you enjoy the book and that it helps you achieve your potential as a footballer.

Paul Broadbent and Andrew Allen

Part 1

Introducing the game

Chapter 1

Playing the game

THIS CHAPTER WILL:
- Explain the principles of play.
- Describe team formations and systems.
- Give an understanding of what it takes to become a goalkeeper.

Principles of play

Playing football is all about attacking and defending, individually and as a team. The principles of playing football depend on whether your team is in possession of the ball, or whether the other team has possession. If your team is in possession of the ball you will be concerned with the **attacking principles of play**. All the players in your team will support the attack, as a unit, with specific responsibilities for each player depending on their individual position and where the ball is at the time.

If your team is not in possession of the football, you will be concerned with the **defending principles of play.** All the players in your team will have defensive responsibilities, as a unit, with specific responsibilities for each

Attack as a team

Defend as a team

player, once again, depending on their individual position and where the ball is.

As a goalkeeper you have an important role to play in both attacking and defending, so it is good to know the principles of play that affect players in all positions.

Attacking principles

Attacking principles of play are about players creating space and then making the most of this space as an individual and as a team. For this to happen, your team needs to be in possession of the football. For it to happen effectively you will need to consider the following points:

- creating space by spreading out – side to side
- creating space by spreading out – end to end
- one-touch play
- changing direction of play
- dribbling.

Creating space by spreading out – side to side

It is important to try to create space both in between and behind defenders and this should happen as soon as possible after your team gains possession. If it is done quickly, it gives the opposition little time to man-mark and cover each other. Players should try to see everything that is happening on the pitch as they spread out, and should not turn their back on the ball. Having stretched out side to side, your team should look to progress forward as quickly as possible.

Creating space by spreading out – end to end

Teams should try to spread out their players 'end to end' as well as 'side to side'. This requires the player furthest away from the ball to make a run towards it, creating space behind them to be used by other players running off the ball into the space. Overlapping runs create space, and can take place on the wings and in central positions.

One-touch play

One-touch play is an extremely effective attacking tactic as it does not allow the opposition time to pressurize you and your team-mates. One-touch play requires players to have an excellent understanding of support and movement on and off the ball. Quick one-touch play, coupled with good movement, can make it very difficult for defenders to mark players and keep a tight formation. The 'wall-pass' is a common one-touch play in football. Passing the ball to a team-mate who plays it back to you, one touch, as you go forward and exploit the space in front of you, is an effective pass for attacking play.

Another example of a one-touch, pass and move play that can be very effective is called 'third man running'. This involves three players – a passer, a receiver and a runner. The ball is played up to the receiver, laid off at an angle to the passer and played one touch into the path of the runner.

Wall-pass

Changing direction of play

Players with the ability to see and then deliver a long diagonal pass from wing to wing can create and set up an opportunity to exploit space. Another effective way of changing the direction of play occurs when players make cross-over runs, pulling defenders out of position and creating space behind them. Another example is reverse passing, with players changing the direction of play by running with the ball in one direction and passing it in the opposite direction.

Dribbling

Dribbling is a very exciting attacking principle and is often used in the last third of the pitch. A player who can take on and beat other players, or draw in defenders, creates space if the ball is delivered at the right time for team-mates to exploit. If a player can take on and go past a defender it also creates a numerical advantage for his team.

Good dribbling can often help to create goals.

Defending principles

Defending principles of play are about denying the team in possession space. The defending team attempts to get all its players back behind the ball, applying pressure to the player in possession both individually and as a team. The following points are crucial to good defending:

- denying the opposition space
- applying pressure
- applying pressure, cover and balance.

Denying the opposition space

Two principles at the heart of good defensive play are **compactness** and **quantity**. In order to prevent the opposition from scoring, the defence has to be organized compactly, blocking the opposition's direct path to goal. Getting players back behind the ball and being compact as a unit makes it harder for the attackers to develop goal-scoring opportunities and generally forces them out to the wings. It is also important for the defending team to get as many players back behind the ball as possible, to outnumber the offensive players. This is why strikers and midfield players need to drop behind the ball when their team loses possession and for full-backs and other defenders to try to delay the attack by 'jockeying' so these players have time to run back.

Applying pressure

Pressurizing the ball is the first principle of defensive play, making it harder for the team in possession to develop their attacking play. Pressurizing the ball is most important when play is close to your own team's goal, to reduce the scoring opportunities. Successfully applying pressure, particularly as a team, often leads to regaining possession. The level of pressure is a decision that needs to be made by a defender in each situation. It may be that the defender needs to 'jockey' the player, delaying and slowing the player down until there are enough defenders to support and cover them. If the player is running with the ball in front of them, it may be appropriate to carry out a well-timed tackle. Applying pressure in whatever form is a team responsibility. Without your team being able to shut or close down the outlet pass, there can be little point in individuals pressurizing the ball. An element of applying pressure involves 'marking' the attacking team players. This could mean staying very close to a specific player, or holding a formation so that if the ball comes into your area you get to the ball before an attacking player. Correct and thoughtful marking of players puts pressure on attacking players and denies them space to play.

Applying pressure, cover and balance

Pressure, cover and balance are the responsibilities of the first, second and third defenders. The **first defender** is the defender who is close enough to the ball to put pressure on the ball, possibly to tackle or to delay the attacker, denying them the opportunity to play the ball forward to their team-mates. This first defender may be a striker in your team. It will all depend on where the ball is at the time. The **second defender**

is any defender who is close enough to cover space behind the first defender, who can step in and defend against the attacker if the first defender is beaten. All other players are **third defenders**. These are defenders who are not close enough to pressure the ball or to cover the space behind the first defender. Third defenders provide 'balance' so that, while other defenders apply pressure to try to win the ball, third defenders cover space on areas of the pitch away from the ball. Third defenders also track runners who run at space behind the defence. Goalkeepers can assist with this role by being a third defender/sweeper, depending on where the ball is on the pitch.

Transition phase

Moving from defence into attack or attack into defence when possession changes is called the 'transition phase'. This can be a crucial part of the game. If a team is slow to get back to defend and set its defensive positions after it has lost the ball, the opposing team can quickly attack on the break, taking advantage of the space left on the pitch. Alternatively, a team that wins the ball and turns defence into attack needs its players to be quick-thinking, making decisive runs into attacking spaces. It is important that all players, in all positions, know their responsibilities as attackers and defenders. Concentration is important, so when there is a change of possession each player knows what his/her role is within the team, so that they act quickly and effectively.

Your role in a team

Whether your team is attacking (in possession) or defending (not in possession) you are likely to have certain responsibilities that will help your team. These responsibilities will vary, depending on the position you play in your team and also depending on where the ball is lost and regained.

Listed below are some of the responsibilities that you will have as a goalkeeper, depending on whether you are attacking or defending.

Attacking

Communicate with your team-mates. You are able to see the whole pitch and can play a part in the attack being effective.

Be prepared to offer support to your defenders by being available for a pass in order to keep possession.

When in possession, think about how quickly your team needs to attack – counter-attack quickly or give your team-mates a few seconds breather to organize themselves.

Make good decisions when distributing the ball: do you pass short or play long?

Defending

Communicate with your defence at all times, organizing them, calling for the ball and passing on information.

Support your defenders by being available to receive their pass back.

Be prepared to come out of your goal area and play with your feet – like having an extra sweeper.

Organize your defence at set plays:corners, free kicks and long throws.

Team formations and systems

Team formations and systems are, in simple terms, how a team lines up at kick off and how they attempt to keep this team shape throughout the game. As a goalkeeper you will have an excellent view of the shape of the team in front of you, and can give advice or support about the formation when necessary. Coaches often ask what 'the best formation' is. There isn't one. A formation is supposed to make best use of the players' abilities within a team. What works best for a team depends on what their strengths are and what kind of players are available. It may also depend on factors such as playing against a strong attacking team or even weather conditions.

Top tips

- A good formation will help a good team, but skill and awareness count for much more.
- Whatever formation your team plays, it is vital that you stay in touch with all team-mates with good communication.
- Be prepared for your formation to change during a game – this decision will be made by your coach rather than the players.

This key applies to all the formations shown in Figures 1.3 to 1.7.

Key

GK	Goalkeeper	LM	Left midfielder
RB	Right-back	CM	Central midfielder
LB	Left-back	CF	Centre-forward
CD	Central defender	LF	Left-forward
RM	Right midfielder	RF	Right-forward

The 4–4–2 formation

The 4–4–2 formation is probably the most common one in the modern game, with a good balance throughout the positions. Four defenders and four midfielders will often mean eight players behind the ball when defending. The four midfielders are also available to support the two forwards when attacking. It can be an effective attacking formation, especially if you have two strong forwards who can outrun the opposition defence, and fast attacking midfielders to support them. However, with only two attackers playing up front, this alone is not enough to stretch apart a defensive line of usually four opponents. The two wide midfielders provide automatic width to the midfield and attacking shape of the team. The use of four defenders adds compactness and balance in the back, where either the sweeper or the flat back four can be utilized.

Figure 1.1 **The 4–4–2 formation**

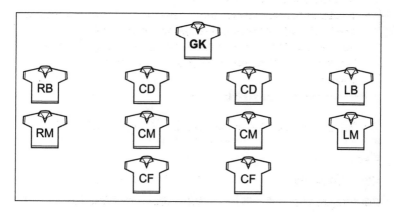

The 3–5–2 formation

The 3–5–2 formation is more attacking than the 4–4–2 formation, as it moves forward the 'fourth full-back', who often may have minimal defending to do against only two attackers. With only three at the back, defenders must be solid and work together as a unit. Often a midfield player may be called upon to support the defence. A coach may consider a 3–5–2 formation if they have an abundance of midfield players. Like all systems it needs to be able to operate when defending and attacking. Using this formation, teams will often defend and attack in two units – the back three and the midfield five when defending, and the midfield five and two forwards when attacking.

Figure 1.2 **The 3–5–2 formation**

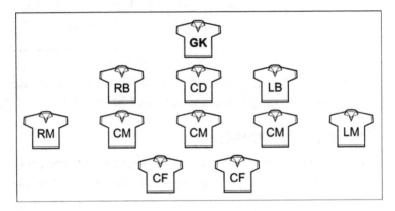

The 4–5–1 formation

The 4–5–1 and 4–3–3 formations are very similar, with the 4–5–1 being a defensive set-up that can easily switch into a 4–3–3 if necessary. The nature of the positioning of the players makes it a very difficult system to break down, particularly if the team remains well organized and disciplined. With the midfield packed and compact, it is good for keeping possession of the ball through a series of short passes, occasionally linking up with the lone forward. In attacking terms there is a real emphasis on the midfield players to get forward to support the lone striker. The wing backs (wide midfield players) provide instant width in attack and good defensive cover in these wide positions. The wing backs

Figure 1.3 **The 4–5–1 formation**

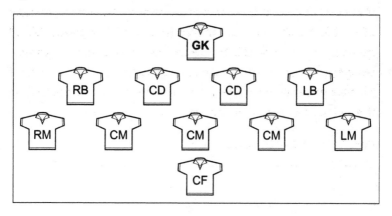

can also be used to bring the ball out of defence. The system may see the back four defenders playing with a sweeper or a 'flat back four'.

The 4–3–3 formation

Teams playing a 4–3–3 formation are likely to be playing a narrow game, through the middle of the pitch, although when the ball is on their side of the pitch, the full-back and wide midfield player should be encouraged to take up wide positions to provide width in the attack. The two full-backs are able to provide automatic width when building play from the back. With 4–3–3, teams need to encourage the wide forwards to drop back to help with the build-up. One of the benefits of this formation for younger players is that they often look to force the ball through the middle of the field, whereas this system encourages them to build attacks by playing the ball forward into the wide channels rather than simply through the middle.

The 3–4–3 formation

The 3–4–3 formation is considered to be an attacking formation when in possession of the ball, and also lends itself to a high-pressure style of

Figure 1.4 **The 4-3-3 formation**

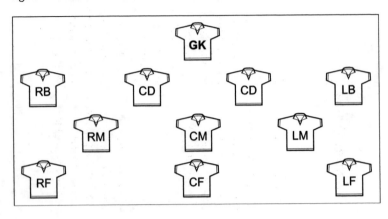

Figure 1.5 **The 3-4-3 formation**

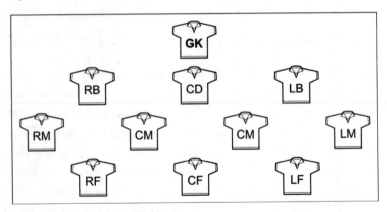

defending without the ball. Using this formation, teams can easily attack and defend with a minimum number of seven players, either the back three and four midfield players when defending, or the midfield four and the three forwards when attacking. Normally the central striker will consistently stay at the tip of the attack while one midfield player will often protect the back three by constantly pressurizing the ball to help the defence.

The advantages and disadvantages of various formations

Table 1.1 **Sets out the advantages and disadvantages of these five systems**

	3–5–2	4–4–2	4–3–3	4–5–1	3–4–3
Defensive strength	Usually one central midfielder sits in front of the back three. This gives good cover of central space.	Four players when defending, provides cover of all space.	Covers the space well. Also good for stopping out opposition playing out from back.	Very strong defensive unit, but does depend on how many players are pushed forward to attack.	Good coverage of the central areas of defence, though without central support from midfield to sit in front of the back three.
Defensive weakness	Three defenders instead of four means 25 per cent extra space for two wide forwards to exploit.	Fewer players in the central areas.	Fewer players in the central areas and less support for full-backs on the transition phase.	Only one forward means the opposition have real opportunity to play the ball in their defensive third.	Even though strong centrally, extra space for two wide forwards to exploit.

Table 1.3 **Sets out the advantages and disadvantages of these five systems**

	3-5-2	4-4-2	4-3-3	4-5-1	3-4-3
Playing out from the back	With only three at the back, wing backs need to drop back, though this then gives them fewer passing options.	The two full-backs start in excellent positions to offer this option to their team.	The two full-backs start in excellent positions to offer this option to their team, though less wide support for the next pass. Often sees teams playing a longer pass forward.	This formation provides several options, though the position will often push a full-back forward into midfield to try to counter this.	With only three at the back it does not offer the options for players to receive the ball in wide positions.
Effect on Midfield	The central midfield area will often have a numerical advantage – three to two.	Provides a diamond or flat shape to the midfield when attacking or defending. If outnumbered in midfield, sometimes a full-back will be pushed into midfield.	The three midfield players are likely to be central, which means the team may require two of the forwards drop back to help in the wider areas of the pitch.	This formation provides several options to the midfield – often three midfield players will support the forward (two wide and one central).	Provides a diamond or flat shape to the midfield. If outnumbered in midfield, it will require one of the forward players to drop back to support the midfield.

Effect on forwards	Provides good central support for runs beyond the forwards.	The midfield and full-backs need to be willing to get forward to support the forwards.	Numerically, it suggests that three forwards offer you more, although this depends on how much dropping back the two wide forwards have to do.	Really needs a forward who is good at holding the ball up and bringing the midfielders into the game.	Numerically it suggests that three forwards offer you more, although this depends on the amount of defensive duties required from the wide forwards.
Overall	Strong centrally and in central midfield. Vulnerable to width at the back.	Strong defensively and can be good for playing out from the back. Best formation for using the full width of the pitch.	Good for stopping opposition's full-backs from playing. Offers less width for playing out from the back, but can offer width in attack.	A relatively defensive formation. The team needs to be able to play well and have a forward who can hold the ball up well.	Strong centrally, in defensive areas, and good formation for using width in midfield. Three forwards provide width in attack.

What it takes to become a goalkeeper

Whatever your favoured position, or the position that you are asked to play in by your coach, you will need a range of technical, physical and psychological skills and attributes. Many of these are relevant to more than one position, for example, a good goalkeeper will need to have the physical and technical ability to play in goal but will also need the technical ability of an outfield player when it comes to controlling and passing the ball.

From research and player observation, it has been identified that 'good goalkeepers' are likely to have the following attributes, most of which can be developed and improved with practice and support from your coach.

- **Technique**
  - quick footwork
  - jumping ability
  - good handling
  - good positioning
  - tackling ability
  - catching technique
  - diving ability
  - goal kicks off the floor and out of hands
  - punching
  - good distribution – throwing and kicking.

- **Physical**
  - strength
  - good balance
  - agility
  - co-ordination
  - speed of movement
  - stamina
  - upper body and arm strength
  - preferably tall – over 1.8 m (5' 11").

- **Mental/**   –   bravery
  psychological –   courage
  - anticipation
  - concentration
  - decisiveness
  - communication
  - determination
  - ability to handle mistakes and criticism
  - confidence.

Quote   'As well as having excellent technical and physical attributes, goalkeepers also have courage and bravery, both vital requirements for playing the position. Courage in taking responsibility, being able to handle pressure and dealing with mistakes and the bravery to put themselves in situations without regard to their own physical safety.'

Simon Smith – goalkeeping coach

Summary

- **Football is all about attacking and defending, and the transition between these. As a goalkeeper you need to understand the attacking and defending principles of play.**

- **You need to be able to control and pass the ball as well as any outfield player.**

- **You need to be clear about your role and responsibilities in the team when you are attacking and when you are defending.**

- A team formation, such as 4–4–2 shows the 'shape' that a team keeps throughout the game. Any formation needs to be flexible and make best use of the players' abilities within a team.

Self-tester

- Give two responsibilities you have when your team is attacking.
- Why does a goalkeeper need the skills of an outfield player?
- What is the role of the 'second defender'?
- What are the advantages of playing a 4–3–3 formation?
- Give three attributes of a good goalkeeper.

Action plan

Using the attributes listed earlier, consider how you match up to the skills and attributes for the position you play. Use this book to find out how you can improve your technique and understanding for the position you play (Chapters 7, 8 and 9 will help you improve your game). With the support of your teacher or coach (and also Chapter 11 of this book), evaluate your performance and develop a goal-setting programme.

Part 2

Preparing for the game

Chapter 2

Fitness for football

THIS CHAPTER WILL:
- Give an understanding of the key elements that make up general fitness.
- Consider the specific elements of fitness that you need as a footballer.
- Outline the importance of exercise to keep fit.

You may know from experience that football can be a physically demanding sport. If you monitored the types of movements that you made during a match it would make an impressive list:

- sprinting
- jogging
- walking
- running backwards
- running sideways
- accelerating
- jumping
- kicking

- turning
- stretching
- diving.

All these will be very difficult if you don't have a basic level of general fitness as well as a specific fitness suited to football.

| Quote | 'Goalkeeping demands physical strength, quick reflexes and total body co-ordination, and remains a challenging position for any 44-year-old grandad!'
Tim Crosby (experienced keeper for Fulbeck United FC) |

The four Ss

Players with good skills, technique and motivation may be 'natural' footballers, but if they are short of general fitness they are unlikely to reach their potential. To be generally fit and healthy and able to do everyday physical activities without feeling tired, you need the four Ss:

- **Speed** – a big part of the game, not just for short sprints but also for longer concentrated spells.
- **Strength** – many skills in football can be helped with physical strength, in both the upper and lower body.
- **Stamina** – football is a high-intensity sport played over a long period and players need to last the full 90 minutes in a match.
- **Suppleness** – flexibility is important because of the wide range of movements required when playing football.

Specific fitness

As well as a good level of general fitness, you need to have specific fitness to play football at a high level. The following are the elements of fitness that can make the difference between a good player and a world-class player:

Figure 2.1 **The four Ss**

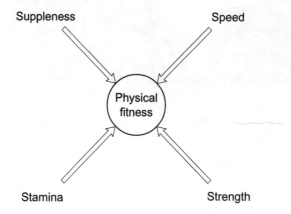

- **Agility** – in a match you turn and change direction many times, as well as jumping and diving, so you need to be able to move and turn quickly and easily.

- **Quick reactions** – you need to respond quickly to constant and sudden changes in play and when making saves.

- **Balance** – when you catch the ball in the air under pressure from opposition players, you need good balance to remain steady and land on your feet.

- **Coordination** – there are a number of different techniques and movements involved in catching, shot stopping and diving to make a save. These rely on different parts of the body working together smoothly and efficiently.

- **Timing** – you need to act at just the right moment, with good timing for your shot stopping and when dealing with crosses.

There are also specific elements of fitness that players in different positions in a team will need. A goalkeeper will certainly have different requirements from a defender, midfielder or striker. However, the crucial physical attributes required by a goalkeeper are speed, strength and suppleness. Speed, linked with timing and quick reactions are vital

when rushing off the line to close down a forward, or quickly to change direction after a shot is deflected. Suppleness is obviously a critical factor for goalkeepers. They need to be flexible enough to stretch for the ball when attempting a save or to dive at a player's feet. Strength is needed whenever there are opposition players in the area around the keeper. They need to command their area and have the power and strength to be first to the ball from corner kicks and crosses into the area. Stamina is not such a crucial attribute, although it is important that keepers have a good general level of fitness so that they are sharp for the full 90 minutes.

Statistics

In the previous two World Cup finals more than 20 per cent of all the goals scored were in the last 15 minutes.

The importance of exercise

Fitness is obviously an important element if you want to play a good standard of football. When you were younger you may not have needed to exercise to keep fit; you naturally used up a lot of energy and kept fit in your daily routines and activities. As you get older, you will notice that you need to work a little harder to keep in good physical condition – and this is where regular exercise fits in. Exercise is good for you. It helps you to develop as a person, both physically and mentally.

On a **physical** level, exercise:

- improves your posture and body shape
- helps cardio-vascular fitness – keeping your muscles supplied with oxygen
- develops your muscle tone and strength
- strengthens your bones
- reduces your chance of illness.

On a **mental** level, exercise:

- helps relieve stress and tension
- increases self-confidence
- gives you a challenge
- gives you something to look forward to – it's fun!

Genetics plays a part; some people need very little exercise to maintain a high fitness level, while others need a daily physical activity to keep fit. Even though some seem to be born with a head start, this doesn't mean that other less naturally fit people cannot see massive improvements providing they train and work hard. If you stop any physical activity for a while, you will definitely notice the difference in your body and your state of mind. Get to know your body and your fitness levels.

- At what times do you feel at your best?
- When do your energy levels feel low?
- How long does it take you to recover from exercise?

The technical bit . . .

Whenever we exercise our respiratory system responds in obvious ways, such as shortness of breath and gasping for air. This is because the body uses more energy as we exercise, and our muscles demand more oxygen to maintain this energy level. The fitter we are through regular exercise, the greater our lung capacity and efficiency, and the less we gasp for breath.

Cardiovascular fitness involves keeping oxygen supplied to your muscles from your heart and lungs. Several things happen to your heart while you exercise. Your heart rate (beats per minute) goes up, increasing the speed at which your heart pumps blood and oxygen, to your muscles. The stroke volume also increases, which is the amount of blood pumped from the heart during each beat. When you are exercising hard, your heart rate can go up to almost three times its resting rate. Well-trained athletes can have a resting rate as low as 30 beats, with most people having a resting heart rate of approximately 60 beats per minute. Reducing the recovery time of your heart rate after exercise to its resting rate is a good sign that you are improving your fitness.

Top tip

Find out how fit you are. Measure your resting heart rate. When you are fully relaxed, find your pulse by placing two fingers over your wrist or the side of your neck and record the number of beats over a minute. Repeat this after some heavy exercise, continuing to measure your heart rate every four or five minutes until you have reached your resting rate. Record the time it took and try it again throughout the season to check if the time increases or decreases.

Statistics

On average a heart beats approximately 86,400 times a day.

Sorting out a training programme

Your performance as a player can be improved by fitness training. There are five general training categories:

- **Aerobic** – endurance training, working your heart and lungs over a long time.
- **Anaerobic** – short, quick, powerful activities to build up muscles.
- **Strength** – weight training, developing specific muscles.
- **Flexibility** – active and passive stretching of muscles.
- **Skills** – improving skills and techniques, supporting specific fitness.

Your training programme is likely to be planned and organized by your coach. It needs to suit you, so make sure you talk to your coach, sharing your views. Answer these questions about yourself, as these will influence the type of programme you could have:

- How fit are you now?
- What exercises do you like?
- Do you have any injuries?
- What exercises do you dislike?
- Do you have any health problems?
- Are there any particular aspects you want to work on (speed, strength, stamina, suppleness)?

Your training will vary for each stage of the year:

- **Pre-season training** – aerobic, anaerobic, flexibility and skills training, with some strength training.

- **Training during the season** – maintain level of general fitness and rest after matches.
- **Recuperation** – rest and relax at the end of the season to recover from any injuries and fatigue, maintain flexibility.
- **Out-of-season training** – aerobic and strength training, maintain flexibility.

It is essential that a coach advises you on any training programme you undertake. They will consider the different fitness components, known as FITT:

Frequency – how often should the type of exercise be performed?
Intensity – how hard should the exercise be?
Time – how long should the exercise session be?
Type – what types of exercises should you use?

With the help of your coach you can develop a weekly programme to support your general and specific fitness. The following is an example of the content of a typical pre-season training programme. This is not in any particular order, and does not include warming up and cooling down.

Aerobic training	5 × 400 metres with 30 seconds recovery or 5–10 km run.
Anaerobic training	10 × 20-metre shuttle followed by 30 seconds rest. 10 × 50-metre shuttle followed by 60 seconds rest.
Strength training	Squat jumps, press-ups, weights/resistance work in a gym.
Flexibility training	Careful stretching for each major muscle group.
Skills training	Working on specific skills.

Summary

- The four Ss are fundamental components of fitness.
- Different playing positions require different physical attributes.
- Exercise has both physical and mental benefits.
- When you exercise, your heart rate (the number of beats per minute) and your stroke volume (amount of blood in each beat) both increase.

Self-tester

- What are the four Ss of general fitness?
- What are the main physical requirements of a goalkeeper?
- Why do we get short of breath when we exercise?

Action plan

Think about a training plan for you for each part of the year. Talk about it with your coach and write it up as a weekly programme. Monitor your fitness each month to check progress.

For more information on fitness, we advise you to read *The Official FA Guide to Fitness for Football* by Dr Richard Hawkins.

Chapter 3

Food for a footballer

THIS CHAPTER WILL:
- Explain the importance of a healthy balanced diet.
- Give an understanding of what to eat and when.
- Examine the place of carbohydrates in a footballer's diet.

Quote | 'You are what you eat.'

This is a well-known phrase that shows the importance of food for our bodies. So what does it mean? It is basically saying that the food you eat has a direct effect on the type of person you are. If you want to lead a healthy lifestyle, stay fit and become physically strong so that you give your best in training and in matches, your diet really does matter.

Nutrients

All living things need food as the basic fuel for life. It keeps us warm, gives us energy and helps us to grow. Our food and drink contains a variety of nutrients, including carbohydrates, fats and proteins. The aim is to try to get the right balance of these each day. Energy-giving foods contain carbohydrates and fats, which are burned up slowly by the body. Energy in food is measured in calories, and a high-calorie diet is needed if you exercise regularly and burn off the calories. Body-building foods that help us to grow are high in protein.

Look at Table 3.1 below to find out a little more about different food types:

Table 3.1 **Food types**

Nutrient	What do they do?	Where do we get them from?
Carbohydrates	These are mainly stored in muscles, as glycogen used for energy. Great demands are placed on these carbohydrate stores during exercise.	Simple carbohydrates (sugars): sweets, cakes, soft drinks. Complex carbohydrates (starches): rice, bread, pasta, potatoes, cereal, fruit.
Fats	These are mainly stored in body tissues and muscles. They help produce energy.	Butter, margarine, oils, oily fish, cheese, whole milk, nuts.
Proteins	These are needed for the growth and repair of body tissues, and to help with the immune system.	Milk, cheese, meat, yoghurt, soya, fish, eggs, nuts.
Vitamins and minerals	These play an important part in being healthy and feeling well.	Present in tiny quantities in natural foods: fruit, vegetables, nuts, fish, meat, eggs, dairy products, cereals.
Fibre	In the digestive system these help absorb and use nutrients.	Wholegrain cereals, fruit, vegetables, seeds, peas, beans.
Water	Performs many functions – essential for healthy living.	Foods, drinks.

A balanced diet

No single food contains all the nutrients we need, so it is important that we eat a wide variety. A balanced diet is one that gives the right mix to keep us healthy and fit. Figure 3.1 shows examples of foods from the main food types, and the recommended proportion to be eaten each day.

Figure 3.1 **The daily recommended requirements of the major food groups**

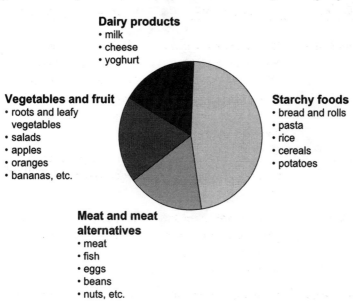

Dairy products
- milk
- cheese
- yoghurt

Vegetables and fruit
- roots and leafy
  vegetables
- salads
- apples
- oranges
- bananas, etc.

Starchy foods
- bread and rolls
- pasta
- rice
- cereals
- potatoes

Meat and meat alternatives
- meat
- fish
- eggs
- beans
- nuts, etc.

Best food for football

When you play football and train regularly you use up a lot of energy, so energy-giving food is needed in your diet. This means that it is best to increase the amount of carbohydrates you eat. Make sure they are mainly 'complex' carbohydrates, such as rice, bread, pasta, cereal and fruit, rather than the 'simple' sugary carbohydrates. The pie charts in

Figure 3.2 **The differences in recommended diet between a normal healthy person and a sportsperson**

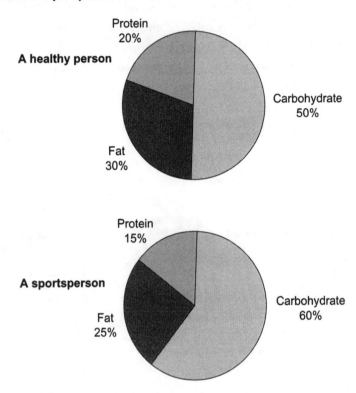

figure 3.2 show the difference in diet between a normal healthy person and that recommended for a sportsperson.

It is recommended that active footballers should get as much as 60–70 per cent of their daily diet in the form of carbohydrates. This is because the carbohydrate stores in your body can run out during exercise.

To ensure that your diet is high in carbohydrate and also 'balanced', a mixture of carbohydrate-rich foods and drinks should be consumed. If you have a good variety it will mean that you will also take in enough of the other nutrients such as protein, vitamins, minerals and fibre. The following foods are rich in carbohydrates:

- breads, pizza bases and crispbreads
- rice, pasta and noodles
- potatoes and potato products
- peas, beans, lentils and corn
- fruit – fresh, dried and tinned
- sugar, jam and honey
- biscuits, cakes and buns
- muesli bars
- yoghurts and puddings
- sports drinks.

Top tip

Think about the types of food you **should** eat when you go shopping for food. Are there any changes you could make?

You need to eat three meals a day, but even then this may not be enough carbohydrate intake if you are active in sport. Therefore, snacking should play an important role in your nutrition programme. The following are popular snacks eaten by footballers as they are high in carbohydrates and relatively low in fat:

- jam, honey, bananas, peanut butter sandwiches
- muesli bars, popcorn
- fruit cake, currant buns, scones
- crumpets, bagels, muffins
- cereal, rice pudding.

Think about the food you eat and the types of snacks you have. Could you alter any of them? Decide on the best times for you to eat snacks. Some footballers like to eat and drink straight after exercise, some like to have a drink and wait an hour or two before eating a snack or meal.

> ## Top tip
>
> Keep up your carbohydrate levels by eating sensibly at meal times and snacking sensibly throughout the day.

The importance of fluids

During training and when playing matches it is vital to drink regularly to maintain hydration. Feeling thirsty is a sign of being dehydrated, but by then it's a little late. By the time you are thirsty you are already partly dehydrated. If you finish a training session and you are thirsty then you have not taken enough fluid on board during the session. Whenever you become thirsty start to drink immediately. Preferably, drink before you are thirsty. Try not to drink too much in one go during a match or training. Drinking too much, too quickly, particularly if already dehydrated, can cause stomach upset.

Drinking plain water is not the most effective way to rehydrate, as drinks should contain moderate electrolyte levels (sodium and some potassium). Sports drinks are a good choice as they are specially made with the correct mix of carbohydrates, fluid and electrolytes.

> ## Top tip
>
> Maintain fluid levels throughout the day by drinking little and often.

Summary

- **Nutrition has an important effect on your overall performance as a footballer.**

- **A balanced diet will ensure you take in enough nutrients to keep you healthy and fit.**

- **Carbohydrate-rich foods need to be eaten to maintain high energy levels while playing matches and training.**

- **Drink enough fluid to stay hydrated.**

Self-tester

- Name five foods that are high in carbohydrates.
- Approximately what percentage of the daily diet of a footballer should be carbohydrates?
- Drinking a lot of water in one go during exercise is the best way to rehydrate. True or false?

Action plan

List the types of food you eat in a week. Check the list against the foods recommended for a balanced diet and one that is rich in carbohydrates. If you need to alter your diet, consider the types of snacks you should eat, and when you should eat them, as well as eating well for the three main meals of the day.

For more information on nutrition, we advise you to read *The Official FA Guide to Fitness for Football* by Dr Richard Hawkins.

Chapter 4

Choosing your kit

THIS CHAPTER WILL:
- Explain the importance of wearing kit that is appropriate for different conditions.
- Give advice on boot maintenance.
- Give guidance on useful equipment to have for training and playing football.

There has been incredible change in the style and manufacture of football kits in the past 50 years. Compared with the heavy, baggy kits of the 1950s, tops and shorts are now lightweight, breathable and very practical. The invention of synthetic fibres, such as nylon, acrylic and polyester made a big difference in this respect. Today, kits are constantly changing, largely due to commercial influences on the game. Gloves and padded tops and shorts have also made a big difference to the comfort and safety of keepers.

Statistics
In the nineteenth century, players often wore caps, and sometimes even top-hats, for matches.

Shirts, shorts and socks

What you choose to play football in is, obviously, down to you. The main consideration is comfort and fit. Make sure that the shorts and top aren't too tight or too baggy, and wear appropriate layers of clothes for the weather conditions. It is important that you are warm enough in cold weather and cool enough in hot weather, and wearing a few thin layers for training is a good way to regulate your temperature. You must also have layers of clothing, such as a tracksuit and waterproofs, to put on if you are a substitute or are substituted during a match. Sudden changes in body temperature once you stop being active need to be regulated by putting on extra layers for warmth. Also, remember that in hot weather, dark tops absorb the heat and will make you feel hotter. You may prefer to wear leggings or tracksuit bottoms, particularly on cold winter days. Make sure they are not too baggy as they may get caught up and interfere with your ball-handling.

Remember that a law of the game is that 'each goalkeeper wears colours which distinguish him from the other players, the referee and the assistant referees', so you should have at least two tops that differ from your team and any others you play against, and possibly a third to avoid conflict with referees.

Football socks are important items to get right as well. Make sure you choose the correct size, wash them regularly and check that they have no rough areas next to your feet. A problem with your feet caused by a poor pair of socks is unnecessary and could cause you foot injuries severe enough to stop you playing for a few weeks. If your socks cause problems then change them for a new pair.

Top tip

If you find that your socks cause problems for your feet, wear a thin pair of cotton socks beneath your football socks.

Football boots

Colour, make, price and style are probably your main reasons for choosing a particular pair of boots. Try to ask yourself a few more questions about the boots before making your selection:

- **Are the football boots comfortable?**
- **Do the boots fit well, especially in the width, with football socks?**
- **Are the boots flexible in all directions, including the bottom of the boot?**
- **Do the boots provide enough protection and support?**

Choose your boots wisely and try them on before buying. One difficult decision you need to make concerns the type of studs to use: screw-in, blades or moulded. The main consideration is the condition and type of surface you will be playing on:

Condition of playing surface	Usual types of studs
Soft ground (SG)	Screw-in or blades
Firm ground (FG)	Moulded or short blades
Hard ground (HG)	Rubber studs or Astroturf™

Screw-in studs

Screw-in studs

Advantages:

- Studs can be changed if they get worn down, so boots last longer.

- Long and short studs are available for some boots, so they can be changed to match the conditions of the pitch.

- Screw-in studs give excellent grip on soft grounds, enabling you to turn, sprint and stop confidently.

- They are a popular type of boot, so there is plenty of choice of style and brand.

Disadvantages:

- There are usually fewer studs than on moulded boots so pressure points and blisters can occur if they are used on hard pitches.

- If you don't check and tighten the studs regularly you can lose them while playing. Even worse, playing with a loose stud can wear out the screw-thread on the boot so that it can never tighten.

> ## Top tip
>
> Put a little grease or lubricant on the screw to ensure the screw/stud does not rust in place.

Moulded studs

Advantages:

- Moulded boots usually have a large number of studs, so the pressure is more evenly distributed on your foot. This minimizes the chance of blisters.

- The studs are shorter than screw-ins, making them more suitable for firm pitches with grip on the top surface.

- Astroturf™ boots are moulded with pimples or small blades and are excellent for artificial grass on training grounds. They are not suitable for grass unless the ground is very hard.

- The football season is getting longer, with tournaments and footy camps continuing throughout the year. This means that you are likely to play on harder pitches during the summer months.

Disadvantages:

- The studs are usually rubber or nylon, and once they are worn down the boots need replacing.

- On wet surfaces or soft ground they provide very poor grip and will definitely affect your performance.

Blades

Advantages:

- There has been a lot of research into the new designs of bladed boots. They claim to provide better turning speed and grip.

- The design means they may be less likely to get stuck in the ground when running.

- Some boots have short and long blades available for different pitch conditions.

- Some blades have replaceable tips so that they can be changed if they become worn or damaged.

Disadvantages:

- If you change from traditional studs to blades they may take a little getting used to as the turning motion is different and does not suit all players.

- There have been some high-profile injuries which have been linked to the design of boots with blades.

Example of bladed studs

Uppers

The top of your boots, or uppers, could be leather or synthetic. In some cases the upper will consist of a mixture of the two. Leather can fit comfortably to the shape of the foot, with a good feel to the ball. However, leather can also stretch when wet and go out of shape. Synthetic boots are generally cheaper than leather ones but have improved in recent years. Many now allow the foot breathe, reducing sweating and making the boot more comfortable to wear. Synthetic uppers are also often used to make a lighter boot.

Choose the boot that is good for you, remembering that comfort is important and so is ball control. The position of the laces now varies, from the traditional top of the foot position to running down the side of the boot. When you try on football boots, decide whether you want the laces off-centre so that they do not get in the way when you strike a ball. Do the boots have a padded tongue that is used to hide the laces, providing a flat surface to strike the ball with? Does the tongue move about or is it secured with velcro or a strap? Also think about the protection that the boot gives your foot. Some lighter boots may offer less protection for the foot but are ideal for fast running as a winger or striker. Other boots may offer good protection but are heavier and may be more suited to you as a goalkeeper.

Statistics

Craig Johnston, the former Liverpool FC player who scored in the 1986 FA Cup Final, is the designer of the 'Predator' football boot.

Looking after your boots

Here are a few tips to keep your boots in good condition. Remember that your boots should not only look good, but also feel good!

- Undo the laces properly when you take your boots off.
- Remove soil by banging the boots together or using a brush, then wipe them with a damp cloth.
- If wet, allow the boots to dry before polishing them or giving them a final clean. Don't dry them near a fire or radiator in case the boots crack or lose their shape.
- Stuffing leather boots with newspaper helps them retain their shape and will help to draw out any moisture from inside the boot.
- Don't play in boots with loose studs, broken studs, mixed studs, or over-tightened studs.
- Don't keep boots in a plastic bag.
- Put your boots on in the dressing room or at the side of the pitch. Walking across car parks or on concrete paths will damage the soles and sharpen the studs or blades.
- Check the boots on a regular basis, looking for any cracks or damage and tightening the studs if necessary.

Gloves

Goalkeeping gloves are designed to protect your hands as well as to provide a better grip on the ball. They now have a huge range of prices and features, but the main things to look for when buying gloves include:

- grip
- protection
- style, comfort and fit
- durability
- wrist support.

Grip

The glove surface is usually latex foam, which sticks to the ball. Smooth foam is generally more 'sticky' than dimpled foam. Some gloves use rubber, which may not grip as well as a foam surface. Check the grip with a wet ball and a dry ball if possible.

Protection

Gloves provide palm cushioning to take the impact of a shot at goal. Thicker foam helps this, but check that it is not so thick that it makes it difficult to grip. The top surface of a glove needs checking also. Does it provide enough protection for punching the ball and is it flexible enough to bend easily? Finger protection is a relatively new feature now found on many gloves. The glove's fingers have plastic inserts that allow the fingers to move forward normally but not bend backwards.

Style, comfort and fit

This will be totally your decision – goalkeepers have their own favourite type of glove and enjoy looking for new features and styles. It is important that you try a range of gloves to compare the feel of different styles and features for comfort and fit. Gloves often look large on a keeper, and many goalkeepers prefer to get a size bigger than they need in order to increase the surface area of the glove. This will depend on your preferences, with some keepers preferring their gloves snug, others liking them a bit larger. If you like close-fitting gloves you may prefer a glove with finger seams sewn on the inside, which are designed for a more snug fit. If you want larger gloves, be very careful that you don't lose the feel of the ball. The gloves should not be so big that your hand moves around inside them or the gloves twist around the hand.

Durability

Gloves may not seem to last long, mainly because they are made from foam. As a guide, thicker foam will usually last longer, as the grip is not just at the surface and holes won't appear at your fingertips. Check the stitching of any new gloves. Poorly made gloves will come apart at the seams before the grip is worn out.

Wrist support

A good pair of gloves will provide some support for the wrist, helping to prevent injury when saving hard shots. Check that your gloves have a wide wrist strap that can be tightened easily and securely.

Looking after your gloves

So, you have spent some time researching and trying out gloves, and now have a pair that is perfect for you. Obviously you need to keep them in top condition, so try to look after them.

- If you want your gloves to last a reasonable length of time, use good goalkeeping technique. Try not to fall on to your hands and, if possible, don't use your hands to get up.

- Wash the gloves regularly to remove dirt and to stop them from smelling. Hand wash them using a little washing powder or soap and rinse them thoroughly with clean water. Let them dry out in the air, not in front of a fire or on a radiator.

- Once the gloves are dry, keep them in a glove bag (many new gloves come with a bag).

- If possible have two sets of gloves, one for practice and one good pair for matches only. When the match gloves get too old, they can become the practice gloves.

- Most foam gloves will grip well if slightly dampened before use. Keep a water bottle in goal for drinking and also for keeping the surface of the gloves moist.

Equipment list

Make sure you check your bag before you leave for any practices or matches. Here's a checklist of the items you may need to take with you:

❏ kit – shorts, top and socks

❏ thin inner socks

❏ warm-up top/bottoms

❏ boots (moulded) for firm ground

❏ boots (screw-in/blades) for soft ground

❏ boot-bag for muddy boots

❏ two pairs of goalie gloves

❏ peaked cap

❏ shin-pads

❏ stud key

❏ extra pair of laces

❏ extra studs for replacements

❏ tape or tie-ups for socks

❏ towel and shower gel (if shower available)

❏ bottle of water/drink

❏ first-aid kit – plasters, elasticated bandage, muscle spray etc.

❏ small bag for valuables.

For practising the drills in this book, equipment lists are provided for each drill. You will generally need a size 5 ball and a supply of, say, eight cones to mark off boundaries for your practice grids.

Summary

- Wear kit to suit the weather conditions.

- A good boot should give you support, stability, grip and traction.

- Choose studs or blades to match the condition of the pitch – use screw-ins or blades for a soft pitch and moulded or short blades for firm pitches.

- Gloves are an important piece of kit for keepers, so check the features carefully and make sure they are right for you.

- Always be prepared for a match, checking that your kit is ready and packed to go.

Self-tester

- What is the law of the game that relates to a goalkeeper's top?
- Which types of studs are better for soft ground?
- What features should you look for when buying a new pair of goalkeeping gloves?

Action Plan

Check the equipment list and make sure you have all you need for training and for matches. Find a suitable box or bag in which to store all the (clean!) equipment so that you are always organized and prepared each time you play football.

Chapter 5

Warming up and cooling down

> THIS CHAPTER WILL:
> - Explain the importance of warming up before a match and at the start of training.
> - Give an understanding of the importance of cooling down.
> - Describe ways to stretch different muscles.

If you go to watch any professional football team playing a match, it is well worth getting to the stadium early to watch the players warming up and stretching. Most teams are out on the pitch 45 minutes before the match, carrying out exercise routines and stretches under the watchful eye of the coach. This is quite a contrast to some local league teams, with players turning up ten minutes before a match and using the run from the changing room to the pitch as their warm-up. Obviously these are two extremes, but this chapter will help to show the importance of a good warm-up and cool down before and after a match, and even during half-time.

Goalkeepers often have their own warm-up and stretching routine before a match, separate from the other players. It may be better to carry out the basic warm-up and stretching with all the players so that you are part of the team in the immediate build-up to the match. Once the match preparation moves from warming up and stretching to ball skills, you can then work on your specific goalkeeping routine using one or two players to help you.

The warm-up

The warm-up is designed to prepare a player for any physical activity, both at training and for a match. Your body needs gradually 'waking-up' from a resting state to a state of readiness to train or play. It is important that the warm-up is gradual, building up from easy walking, movement of joints and jogging, through to sprinting and quick turning. Ideally you want a warm-up to match your movements in a game so that similar muscles and joints are prepared for action. In the warm-up, use exercises such as side-strides, sharp turns and jumping, as well as ball control, catching, diving and passing. These exercises will not only prepare muscles and joints, but will also have the advantage of ensuring the effect is on those muscles used for playing football, so helping to prevent injuries. Warming up with a football 'tunes you in' to football skills, preparing you mentally for the game, and gives you the chance get a feel for the playing surface.

Statistics

The recommended time for warming up is between 15 and 25 minutes, completing the warm-up approximately 5–10 minutes before a match.

The main purposes for warming up are:

- **to raise body temperature**
- **to increase muscle temperature**
- **to reduce muscle tightness**

- to help achieve joint mobility
- to prepare the cardiovascular and respiratory systems
- to decrease the risk of injury
- to prepare mentally for physical activity.

The technical bit . . .

The term 'warm-up' implies the key objective of raising body and muscle temperature. As muscles contract they use up energy. Less than a quarter of this energy goes towards producing mechanical work, with the rest of the energy generating heat within the muscle cells. By moving muscles, their performance is improved as their temperature rises. However, this is only one part of improving their performance: raising body temperature by just one degree Celsius is enough to maximize the effect on the active muscles. It has been found that the best way to generate the necessary internal heat is by running.

Mobility and flexibility

Warming up helps you to keep mobile and flexible, through moving your joints and stretching.

- Mobility is the amount of movement your joints will allow.
- Flexibility is the amount of 'stretch' your muscles allow as you move.

Flexibility exercises increase the stretching potential of the muscles, improving movement. Daily stretching is important, so use the examples on the following page to work out a routine.

Good mobility is essential for sprinting, turning, jumping and diving. Before any sudden twisting or explosive movements, you need to move your joints in a slow smooth action. Preparing your back and neck is particularly important before any exercise.

Good mobility helps you to turn quickly.

Joint rotations

From a balanced, standing position, with your arms hanging loosely at your sides, bend, extend, and rotate each of the following joints. Perform eight to ten rotations for each group of joints before moving on to the next group:

- fingers
- wrists
- elbows
- neck
- back and shoulder blades
- hips
- knees
- ankles
- feet and toes.

Work through this sequence of rotations slowly and smoothly, and think about the movements that occur at each joint. Complete the series of joint rotations from fingers to toes in no more than three to four minutes.

Statistics

You begin to lose natural mobility and flexibility from the age of eight, so all players need to know how to work on muscles and joints.

Stretching

Correct stretching of your muscles each day, and especially before training and matches, is important to help avoid injuries and to improve flexibility and performance. Stretching is quite 'static', so it needs to be part of an active warm-up. Common sense and some thought is needed to make the stretching effective:

- Don't over-stretch or put too much strain on your muscles. If there is any pain – stop and find a different position. Stretching shouldn't be painful, just hold a stretch up to a point of tension.

- Don't stretch if your muscles are very cold – warm them up first and also get your joints mobile by rotating and moving wrists, hips, knees etc.

- Start with very gentle stretching, and make each movement slow. Hold a stretch for 10–15 seconds and slowly release, repeating several times.

- Don't 'bounce' into a stretch – you need to control the movement.

- Be systematic so you don't miss out any particular muscle group.

Top tip

Try to develop a daily stretching routine. Spend a few minutes in the morning gently stretching key muscles – it will increase your flexibility and help avoid injuries. Animals such as cats and dogs enjoy a good stretch after waking up – and look at their flexibility!

Try the following stretches for the major muscle groups of the body.

Figure 5.1 **Major muscle groups**

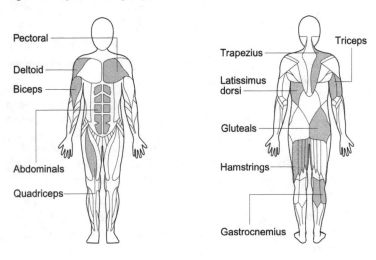

Calf stretch

Facing a wall or partner, step forwards onto a bent left leg. Increasing the weight on your hands, deepen the left leg bend and straighten your right leg back. You should feel the stretch at the top of the calf on the right leg. Try to make the heel of your right leg touch the ground but don't force it. Hold it for ten seconds and repeat three or four times for each leg.

Figure 5.2 **Calf stretch**

Quads stretch

Stand to the side of a wall or use a partner for balance. Gently raise one heel up behind you by grasping the ankle with your hand. Feel the stretch in the quadriceps just above the knees. Repeat with the other leg.

Figure 5.3 **Quads stretch**

Hamstring stretch – standing

Straighten one leg in front of you and slightly bend the other leg. Place both hands on the thigh of your bent leg and sit back gently. Don't bounce. Hold it for 10–15 seconds and then change legs.

Figure 5.4 **Hamstring stretch – standing**

Hamstring stretch – lying down

Lie on your back with your legs out flat. With your hands holding behind your left knee, raise your leg at the hip, with the knee still bent at 90 degrees. Hold this position and then slowly raise your leg at the knee joint until a stretch can be felt in the hamstring muscles. Relax and repeat three or four times for each leg.

Figure 5.5 **Hamstring stretch – lying down**

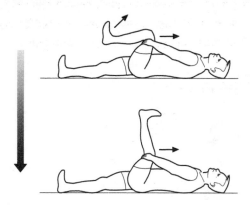

Gluteal stretch

Sit on the ground with knees pointing skywards. Cross your left leg over your right so it is resting behind the knee. Gently push the crossed leg towards your chest with the help of the other leg, but don't push too far. Repeat for other leg.

Figure 5.6 **Gluteal stretch.**

Groin inward stretch

Sit on the floor with your knees bent and lean back on your hands. Slowly push one leg in and downward until you feel a little strain on your thigh. Hold it for 5–10 seconds, release and repeat four times on each leg.

Figure 5.7 **Groin inward stretch**

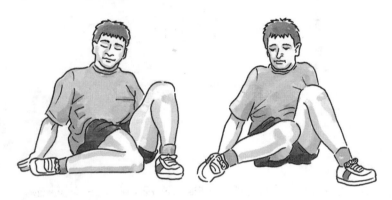

Groin outward stretch

Stand with legs wide apart and weight even, knees slightly bent and hands on hips. Increase the bend in one leg and straighten the other by sliding it out so you take a sideways lunge. Don't bounce, and don't bend the knee of the bent leg beyond the foot position.

Figure 5.8 **Groin outward strech**

Back stretch

Lie on your back and bring in your hips and knees until your knees touch your chest. Put your hands on your knees and gently pull them towards your chest, lifting your hips slightly. Lift your head carefully and slowly off the ground until you feel a slight stretch in your back.

Figure 5.9 **Back stretch**

Side stretch

Stand upright and balanced. Reach your left hand up and over your head, bending slowly to your right. Slide your right hand down your right leg as you bend. Keep your hips still and your weight evenly balanced as you bend. Don't bounce. Repeat this stretch for the other side.

Figure 5.10 **Side stretch**

Stomach stretch

Lie on your back with your arms stretched up over your head on the ground. Stretch as far as you can, with your toes pointed forwards and fingers reaching back. Hold the stretch for 30 seconds.

Figure 5.11 **Stomach stretch**

Triceps stretch

With your back straight, raise one arm and drop it over your shoulder. Reach down your back, feeling the stretch in the upper arm. Repeat with other arm.

Figure 5.12 **Triceps stretch**

Deltoid stretch

Sit up straight with right arm bent behind you, hand flat against your back. Use the left hand to ease your right arm across your back and reach up with the right hand towards the middle of the shoulder blades. Feel the stretch in the outer shoulder.

Figure 5.13 **Deltoid stretch**

Pre-match routine

It is a good idea to have a set routine of goalkeeping drills before a match, so that you know that you have practised and prepared for all the different situations that may arise in the match. Once you have warmed up and stretched, move to the goal with one or two 'servers' (any substitutes are usually willing to help) and try to include the following types of activities. For each activity, visualize the movements and picture yourself using them in the match, so you are fully prepared and full of confidence.

On the spot

Quick feet are important, so include some sort of explosive foot movement. Jog on the spot and then sprint hard on the spot, pumping your arms for five seconds. Relax into a jog and repeat. Continue this, varying the quick feet movement:

- move in a 'figure of 8' on the spot
- sprint and end with a jump
- sprint with knees up.

Warm up the hands

Stand in front of the goal. From around the penalty spot a server strikes the ball at you at varying heights. This is to warm up the hands and to get a feel for the ball, so the server isn't trying to beat you and score. Roll it back to the server underarm so that the warm-up is continuous and dynamic.

Bouncing ball

Get used to the bounce in the area. Ask a player to 'bounce pass' the ball to you with an overarm throw at a varying pace and height.

Changing the angle

Servers start at the touchline on the edge of the area and strike a low ball and then a medium/high ball to you. Make sure you are standing at the correct position and angle to save the shot. The players move around the edge of the area, changing the angle of shot until they reach the other side of the area. They take six to eight shots, and you need to make sure that you are prepared, getting the angles right for each shot.

Diving

Ask the servers to strike the ball just to your left and right to practise diving. Decide whether to catch or parry each shot, and repeat this on both sides six to eight times.

Crosses

Use a server on each side, near the touchline. Ask them to put in crosses for you to catch or punch out. Make sure the crosses vary in height and pace.

Throwing and kicking

Stand a server near the half-way line, towards the touchline, and throw or kick the ball out to them. Concentrate on accuracy and technique for the overarm throw and the drop kick or goal kick. Ask the server to come closer to practise clearances from back passes.

A warm-up programme

Before each match and at the start of training, your coach is likely to plan a programme for warming up, which includes stretching. It is always a good idea to stretch once your muscles have warmed up a little, after an initial jog.

Below is an outline of a programme that can be adapted for your use before a match:

Activities	Duration/distance
1 Jog – very easy pace across pitch and back twice.	4 × 50 metres
2 Joint rotations – slow circular movement of all joints: ankles, knees, hips, wrists, elbows, shoulders. Gentle neck and back movements.	3 minutes
3 Jog – cruising pace across pitch and back twice. Try to include: • normal run • side-strides • running backwards • cross-steps during run.	4 × 50 metres
4 Stretching – light stretching (quads, hamstrings, groin, back) as well as any specific stretches you feel help.	5 minutes
5 Goalkeeping drills, with 'servers' • on the spot • warm up the hands • bouncing ball • changing the angle • diving • crosses • throwing and kicking.	15 minutes

Warming down

Cooling or warming down is seen as essential in many other sports such as athletics, swimming and cycling, but it is only in recent years that it has become part of the routine after football matches. It is often easier to fit in a warm-down after training than after a match because all the players are still wound up in the emotions of the game they have just played. However, warming down after a match should be part of your routine if you want to look after your body.

The most important thing is that a warm-down is active but gentle. You are aiming to return your heart rate and respiration gradually back to normal, and to allow the waste products (lactic acid) from the muscles to be reabsorbed. If you cool down too quickly at the end of a match or training, particularly if you have been working very hard, you are more likely to suffer from muscle stiffness caused by a build-up of lactic acid. The graph in figure 5.14 shows the importance of an active warm-down.

Immediately after a match, take a few minutes' rest. Your coach may wish to talk to you and this is when you will share the experience of the match with your team-mates. It is important that you take in fluids to start rehydration at this stage. The best form of warm-down is jogging at an easy pace for several minutes, going down to a walk. Ten minutes' warm-down is enough to have a positive effect.

Figure 5.14 **Levels of lactic acid after activity (Bangsbo1994)**
Source: *Fitness Training in Football – A Scientific Approach*, Jens Bangsbo (Ho & Storm) (1994)

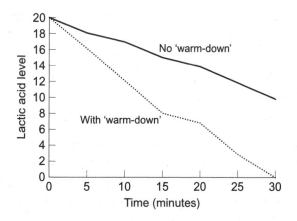

Gentle stretching can also be part of the warm-down. It helps bring your body back towards a state of rest and recovery and allows you to focus on relaxing and lengthening the muscles that you have put under stress during the match or training session.

Top tip

Warm down after each match or training session with a gentle jog and stretch. Not only will it ease any muscle aches, but it has also been shown to improve your sleep in the immediate nights that follow.

Summary

- **Warming up and warming down need to be part of your routine before and after matches and training.**

- **Stretching is important to maximize performance and reduce the risk of injury.**

- **Make stretching and joint movement part of a daily routine.**

- **Work out a pre-match routine of warming up and preparation for the match.**

Self-tester

- Give three reasons for warming up before a match.
- Describe a stretch for your hamstring.
- Why is it a good idea to have a pre-match routine of goalkeeping drills?

Action plan

Plan a warm-up routine for yourself before a match or training session. Think about a balance of exercises for the different parts of your body, and drills for the different goalkeeping situations. Get into the habit of stretching muscles and moving joints as a routine each day.

For more information on warming up and cooling down, we advise you to read *The Official FA Guide to Fitness for Football* by Dr Richard Hawkins.

Chapter 6

Dealing with injuries

THIS CHAPTER WILL:

- Describe the different sorts of injuries that you may be unlucky enough to get as a goalkeeper.
- Outline ways to help you prevent injuries.
- Explain the basic treatments that are needed for different injuries.

Football is a high-energy, body-contact sport, so at some stage in your football career you will get an injury. Don't let this put you off, though! The more informed you are about the different types of possible injuries and the ways to avoid and treat them, the more chance you have of getting through each season with fewer injury problems.

Statistics

A total of more than 3,000 injuries are suffered each season by the 2500 or so professionals in the Premier League and Football League. Each injury keeps a player out of the game for an average of four matches.

The information in this chapter is only for guidance and general interest. If you are concerned about any injuries you have, and certainly if the injury is serious, you must seek medical advice from your doctor or visit a hospital.

Types of injury

There are two different types of sporting injury: **chronic** and **acute**. The causes for these make each type distinctive.

Chronic injuries

These are caused by continuous stress on a particular part of the body over a long period of time. Examples for other sports include tennis elbow or golfer's elbow. There are fewer chronic injuries involved with football, but if you overuse a particular part of the body for too long you may develop a chronic injury. A possible problem from running long distances in training is an injury called 'shin splints'. Symptoms include:

* **tenderness on the inside of the shin**
* **lower leg pain**
* **possible swelling**
* **pain when the foot is bent downwards**
* **a slight redness to the shin.**

If you suffer from this, the main thing to do is rest. You can apply ice in the early stages when it is very painful, but the sooner you rest the sooner it will heal. To prevent chronic injuries, train carefully, rest between training sessions, wear good footwear and improve your technique.

Acute injuries

These are caused by a sudden stress on the body and are more common than chronic injuries in football. They can include bone fractures, pulled muscles, concussion or bruising. It is useful to separate these types of injuries into soft-tissue and hard-tissue injuries.

Soft-tissue injuries

These include:

- open injuries where the skin is broken, such as cuts, grazes and blisters

- closed injuries that happen beneath the skin, including:

  - bruises – blood vessels are damaged
  - strains – pulled muscles and tendons from torn tissue
  - sprains – ligaments stretched or torn at a joint, such as an ankle
  - dislocation – bone pulled out of its normal position at a joint, e.g. finger
  - torn cartilage – damage to the cartilage around a joint such as the knee.

Statistics

The most common type of injury in football, by a long way, is muscle strain. This accounts for about one-third of all injuries.

Hard-tissue injuries

These injuries are bone fractures. They could be cracks in the bone, or an actual break. With a fractured bone there is likely to be bruising and swelling, as well as a great deal of pain because of the damaged nerves inside the bone.

Treating injuries

The majority of the injuries you will get through playing football will be minor soft tissue injuries, such as sprains, strains and bruises. The RICE method is a good way to treat these:

R   rest $\rightarrow$ stop immediately and rest the injury.
I   ice $\rightarrow$ apply ice to the injury to make the blood vessels contract and reduce swelling.
C   compression $\rightarrow$ put on a bandage (not too tight) to help reduce swelling.
E   elevation $\rightarrow$ raise the injury to reduce the flow of blood.

Anything more serious than a minor soft-tissue injury will need proper medical attention. This includes any fracture, dislocation or torn cartilage, or any injury to the head.

Looking after your feet

Feet are obviously a key part of the body when playing football, and yet foot-care advice is largely ignored by many footballers. Infections and painful problems can result if simple advice isn't followed, possibly preventing you from training and playing.

Blisters

Blisters are layers of the outer surface of the skin separated from one another, caused by twisting or friction on the feet. The empty space between the separated skin layers is often filled with fluid. If this fluid contains blood, this signifies a deeper blister that will need treatment to stop infection.

Prevention

To help prevent blisters:

- ensure correctly fitting footwear
- introduce the wearing of new footwear slowly
- wet and 'stretch' areas of footwear that may cause friction
- wear thin cotton socks, perhaps sweat-absorbent ones, under football socks
- try applying Vaseline or other similar 'second skins' on areas of the foot liable to friction.

Treatment

To treat blisters:

- clean the area with antiseptic cream or lotion
- apply cotton-backed tape and a large foam pad over the area, with a hole cut to the size of the blister.

Calluses

These are caused by excessive friction and pressure, resulting in a thickening of the skin. They are tender and painful to touch.

Prevention

To help prevent calluses:

- ensure correctly fitting footwear
- wear thin cotton socks, perhaps sweat-absorbent ones, under football socks
- make sure you don't have a problem with the alignment of your foot – see a doctor or podiatrist to check this.

Treatment

To treat calluses:

* visit a podiatrist or chiropodist who will trim the calluses, so relieving the pressure
* consider changing your footwear to give a better fit
* correct your foot alignment if this is diagnosed as a problem.

Athlete's foot

This is caused by a fungus and can spread very quickly. This is particularly the case if players walk around barefoot in changing rooms with contaminated floors. It commonly occurs between the toes, where the white skin becomes white and scaly. It is usually itchy and you may feel a burning sensation.

Prevention

To help prevent athlete's foot:

* wear flip-flops in changing rooms and shower areas
* use footbaths
* dry between your toes after washing, and apply talcum powder if necessary
* don't share towels or socks with other players.

Treatment

To treat athlete's foot:

* consult a doctor or pharmacist
* use the prescribed anti-fungal cream, lotion or powder regularly until the infection goes
* keep the toes clean, dry and out in the air during this period.

Ingrowing toenail

Problems may occur if you cut your nails too short, or cut down into each corner. This may cause a red swelling of the skin and a discharge from the nail bed around the edge of the nail. In extreme cases you may get an ingrowing toenail, when the nail, or a ragged nail spike, grows down into the skin at the side of the nail.

Prevention

To help prevent ingrowing toenails:

*   ensure correctly fitting footwear
*   keep your nails cut even and short, but not too short
*   don't cut down into the corners of your nails
*   use a file to smooth the edges of your nails.

Treatment

If the area around the nail is painful, inflamed and red or has a discharge of fluid, then consult a doctor, podiatrist or chiropodist.

Top tip

One of the main causes of foot problems, including ingrowing toenails, blisters and calluses, are badly fitting shoes, boots or trainers. Choose your footwear carefully, for comfort, not brand, making sure that they are not too tight or too loose.

Getting cramp and stitch

Cramp

Some people suffer with this more than others, but if you've ever had cramp during a match you'll know it is very painful and makes it almost impossible to continue playing. Your muscle contracts or spasms, with a feeling as if it has 'locked up'. Fortunately it usually goes off after a while, but if you suffer with cramp consistently it may be a good idea to consult your doctor about it. Why it happens is still partly unknown and based on different theories. It is probably caused by a number of factors, including:

- dehydration
- overheating
- a lack of blood flowing to the muscles
- a lack of salt minerals in the blood
- a build-up of lactic acid in the muscles.

Prevention

To help prevent cramp:

- drink plenty of fluids
- eat a diet that is suitable for a footballer (see pages 37–40)
- warm up and stretch well before the match (see pages 57–72)
- rehydrate with fluid at half-time.

Treatment

To treat cramp:

- take the weight off the affected muscle
- carefully stretch the muscle and hold it in a stretched position
- massage the muscle gently to relax it and get the blood flowing
- drink an isotonic drink to make up for the salt mineral loss.

Stitch

Stitches are likely to be caused by a muscle cramp of the diaphragm – the muscle that helps us breathe. When we inhale we move the diaphragm down, when we exhale (breathe out) it moves up. The diaphragm is positioned between the chest cavity and the abdominal cavity, with the internal organs in the abdomen connected to the diaphragm. During running these organs are bounced around and pull down on the diaphragm as we exhale, causing a stitch. Interestingly most people get a stitch on the right side which is where the largest organ, the liver, is located.

Prevention

To help prevent stitch:

- breathe deeply when running
- try to relax your chest and stomach.

Treatment

To treat stitch:

- stop exercising for a short while
- take deep breaths
- breathe out slowly.

Top tip

If you get a stitch while running, try breathing out as your left foot hits the ground. The organs on your left side are smaller than on the right side so this may reduce the effect of a stitch.

Preventing injuries

Many minor injuries sustained during a football match or training session can be avoided. This is particularly true for foot problems.

Before the game

Before any match or training session, make sure you:

- check that your feet are in good condition, with nails cut and any blisters or other problems treated
- take off watches and jewellery etc.
- check that the area you are practising or playing on is free from glass and stones

- warm up correctly, preparing your muscles and joints (see pages 57–72)
- wear comfortable, well-fitting trainers or boots
- wear a thin pair of cotton socks under your football socks
- check that the stud length suits the condition of the pitch
- use a good pair of shin-pads.

During the game

Make sure you:

- use the correct technique for catching, diving, kicking and passing
- keep warmed up if you are a substitute
- keep your fluid levels up by having a drink at half-time.

After the game

Be sure to:

- cool down properly (see pages 72–74)
- rest properly to give yourself good recovery time before playing again.

Statistics

Approximately one-third of injuries are sustained during training, while the remaining two-thirds occur during matches.

Summary

- **Chronic injuries are caused by overuse over time. Acute injuries are more common in football and are caused by sudden stress.**

- **Most acute injuries in football are minor soft-tissue injuries, such as bruising, strains and sprains. Hard-tissue injuries are bone fractures.**

- **The RICE method is a good way to treat minor soft-tissue injuries.**

- **Look after your feet!**

- **Try to prevent injuries and problems before they occur.**

Self-tester

- Give an example of a chronic sporting injury.
- What does RICE stand for?
- What are the best ways to prevent blisters?
- Describe the probable cause of a stitch.

Action Plan

List the injuries and problems, however minor, that you have had in the past few years through playing football. For each injury write down possible ways these could have been avoided. Use this to give yourself a checklist of things to do to help prevent or limit injuries in the future.

Part 3

Improving your game

Chapter 7

Football fundamentals

THIS CHAPTER WILL:
- Outline some of the basic skills required by all young footballers, irrespective of what position they are playing in.
- Give technique tips that will help players understand these basic skills.

There are certain basic skills that all footballers need to develop and practise. Football is a team game, where passing the ball is an essential part of keeping the ball and developing attacking play. All players need to pass the ball competently and confidently, with goalkeepers passing the ball far more now than in the past. Controlling the ball from a pass is another basic skill that can be practised. Having a good first touch looks an effortless skill from top professionals, but it requires excellent technique and great concentration. Passing and ball control are two skills that you, as a goalkeeper, need to practise with the other players in your team, to help you become a good all-round player.

Passing

Passing is the most frequently used of techniques in the game of football. Coaches will often say 'if you can't pass the ball you can't play', which is why passing is one of football's fundamentals. Without the ability to pass the ball accurately and precisely your team will struggle to keep possession and build up attempts on goal.

Being able to pass the ball is absolutely fundamental.

A good player will have a wide range of passing techniques, using different parts of the foot surface. These include:

- the inside of the foot
- the outside of the foot
- the instep of the foot
- the toe
- the sole of the foot
- the heel of the foot.

You will also need to consider the different passing options:

- **Do you need to make a short pass?**
- **Does the ball need to travel a long distance?**
- **Do you want to pass in the air or on the ground?**

These decisions help you to choose the type of pass to make. You also need to consider the following important elements:

- **whether to disguise the pass**
- **the speed or weight of the pass**
- **the timing of the pass**
- **the accuracy of the pass.**

When a player can effectively and regularly deliver on these elements, they will be considered a good passer of the ball for their team.

Top tip

A good pass is one that arrives just in front of the receiver so they can take the ball without breaking stride and move up field to build their team's attempt on goal – which is an attacking principle of play and the main objective of being in possession.

Although there are many passing techniques that you can practise, this section considers three of the most common passes used in the modern game:

- **the push pass**
- **the low driven pass**
- **the lofted pass.**

The push pass

The push pass is the most commonly used pass at all levels of football. For passes up to approximately 25 metres, the push pass is also the most accurate.

The technique

You should approach the ball at a slight angle, with your non-kicking foot placed alongside the ball. Be careful not to get too close as this will prevent you from swinging your kicking leg freely. The ankle of the passing foot should be kept firm. The ball is then passed using the inside of your kicking foot, making contact through the middle of the ball. For accuracy you should follow through in the same direction as the target of the pass. At all times the head remains steady with eyes fixed on the ball.

A push pass is the most accurate type of pass.

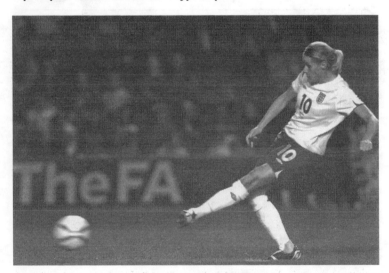

A low driven pass will travel a greater distance.

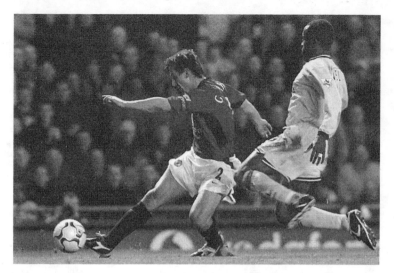

The low driven pass

A common pass for footballers to master is the low driven pass. It allows players to pass the ball over longer distances and also at a greater pace, so that the ball reaches the receiver in a shorter period of time.

The technique

The technique is similar to the push pass, but with modifications at the point of striking the ball. You should approach the ball at a slight angle with your non-kicking foot placed alongside the ball. For this pass, however, the standing foot needs to be slightly in front of the ball. Be careful not to get too close, as this will prevent you from swinging your kicking foot freely through the ball. Your passing foot ankle should be firm.

The ball is then passed with the kicking foot making contact through the middle of the ball. The kicking foot needs to fully extend down so that the pass is made using the laces of the boot. Once again, the follow-through is important and should follow the line of the intended target. At all times the head remains steady, with eyes fixed on the ball.

The lofted pass

When players are choosing their passing options, one thing they will need to consider is whether to pass the ball on the ground or in the air. If the opposition have players in between the passer and the team mate being passed to, then one option is to try the lofted pass. This will take the ball over the head of the defending player and hopefully into the path of the attacker.

The technique

You approach the ball at a slight angle and plant your standing foot alongside the ball, but this time slightly behind the ball. Your last stride into the ball will be longer than previous strides. This allows you to increase the length of the back-swing on your kicking foot. You must not plant your standing foot too close to the ball or it will interfere with swinging your kicking leg freely. Similar to the low driven pass, the point of contact with the ball is made through the laces (the instep) of the boot. However, with this particular pass the contact is made with the underside of the ball. Although it is still important to keep the head steady with eyes fixed on the ball, the body position should be slightly leaning back. The length of the back-swing of the kicking foot and the pace of the follow-through increases the distance of the pass. For accuracy, it is important that the follow-through is in line with the intended target.

Top tip

Remember to practise your techniques using both feet, not just the foot you prefer.

A lofted pass will take the ball over the head of the defending players.

Ball control

If you watch top players, you will soon notice how comfortable they are when receiving the ball. They are concerned about what they are going to do next, rather than about receiving the ball. Ball control is another football fundamental and something all good players will have spent hours practising on the training ground. You can gain or lose vital seconds depending on how good you are at controlling the ball. As soon as the ball is under control, players quickly consider what to do next. Do they:

- **look to run with the ball?**
- **look to dribble?**
- **try to shoot?**
- **try to pass the ball to a team-mate? (This is the most common option.)**

You therefore need to practise getting the ball quickly under control so that you can keep possession of the ball for your team and develop the attacking play. There are four surfaces of the body that you can use to control the ball:

- the feet
- the thigh
- the chest
- the head.

Top players can control the ball with ease.

For the purposes of this chapter we will concentrate on the basic techniques for controlling the ball with the feet, thighs and chest.

Top tip

Players should look to play their first touch away from their body and into a position that will allow them to immediately consider their options – whether to run with ball, dribble, shoot or pass, on their second touch.

Whatever surface is chosen to control the ball, there are real advantages of playing the ball out and in front of the body with the first touch. By doing this:

- you will gain time to consider options, as the ball is not stuck under the foot
- you will improve your vision for passing/shooting options as your head is likely to be up
- your accuracy will be improved as a vital gap is created between your feet and the ball to help effective technique.

There are two basic types of ball control, the **cushion control** and the **wedge control.** Both can be used by all the different surfaces, though the techniques in this chapter concentrate on the following:

- cushion control using the inside of the foot
- cushion control using the top of the foot
- cushion control using the thigh
- cushion control using the chest
- wedge control using the feet.

Cushion control using the inside of the foot

The technique

It is important to be well balanced when you are receiving the ball, so you must move into the line of the ball as early as possible. This gives you less chance of being caught off balance. Decide which foot you will be controlling the ball with and watch the ball onto the side of your foot. As the ball meets your foot, immediately pull back or withdraw the inside of the foot. This will provide a cushioning effect and should leave the ball close to your foot but slightly ahead of you, so you can choose your next option with your second touch.

If you do not withdraw on impact, the ball is likely to bounce away from you and into the path of the opposition. The head should remain still throughout, with eyes fixed on the ball.

Cushion control using the inside of the foot

Cushion control using the top of the foot

The technique

Once again it is important to be well balanced when you receive the ball. For this reason there are advantages to getting into line with the ball as early as possible so you are not stretching for the ball. Decide which foot you will be controlling the ball with and watch the ball onto the foot. For this technique it is likely to be your preferred kicking foot, as it is a slightly more difficult technique than using the inside of the foot.

As the ball meets your foot, on the laces of your boot, immediately withdraw or pull back your foot. You should see the ball cushioned and resting just in front of you. If the ball is a comfortable distance from your body then your second touch can be a pass, shot or dribble. The head should remain still throughout the practice with eyes fixed on the ball.

Cushion control using the top of the foot

Cushion control using the thigh

The technique

With all the ball control techniques it is important to be well balanced and composed as you receive the ball. The best chance of this happening is to get in line with the ball as quickly as possible. Depending on the flight of the ball and your positioning, you will need to select which thigh you are going to use to control the ball. After offering your thigh to the ball, as soon as contact is made, withdraw your leg. This should provide the cushioning effect for the ball to rest close to your feet, but just far enough away from you so your next touch can be a pass, dribble or shot. Keep your head still throughout with your eyes fixed on the ball. The ball will bounce away from you if you do not withdraw your thigh on impact with the ball.

Cushion control using the thigh

Cushion control using the chest

The technique

This technique is very similar to the previous three techniques, with the same principles applying. Be well balanced when receiving the ball. Get in line with the ball as quickly as possible and watch the ball onto the chest, with your head remaining steady. As the ball makes impact with your chest, try to withdraw the surface by leaning back slightly. This will see the ball bounce up a little, but will provide the cushioning impact which will allow the ball to drop down near your feet to let you play your second touch. In order to lean back, you will need to bend your knees. You will find that spreading your arms out slightly may help with balance and can also help to shield the ball if marked by a defender.

Cushion control using the chest

Top tip

Cushion control is the most common way of bringing a ball under control. Whichever part of the body you use, the principle is the same: withdraw your controlling surface at the point of impact to stop the ball bouncing away.

Wedge control using the feet

The technique

This is slightly more difficult technique to master than cushion control. With cushion control you withdraw or pull back the surface on impact with the ball. The wedge control is the opposite movement: immediately on impact you redirect the ball away from your body and into the available space. This technique of controlling the ball is more likely to be used if you do not have so much time to receive the ball. As with the cushion control, it is important to be well balanced when you are receiving the ball, so you must move into the line of the ball as early as possible. Decide which foot you will be controlling the ball with and watch the ball onto your foot. You can use either the inside or outside of the foot for the first touch. As the ball meets your foot, immediately jab or push down so that the ball does not go too far away from you, but is played away into space.

Summary

- **Goalkeepers need to be confident passers of the ball, using a variety of techniques to keep the ball in possession by passing accurately to team-mates**

- **Ball control, by cushioning the ball or using wedge control, is an essential basic skill for goalkeepers to practise and develop.**

Self-tester

- Describe the technique used for a push pass.
- Is your body position leaning forward or back for a lofted pass?
- For cushion control with your foot, do you withdraw or pull back your foot on impact, or do you move your foot towards the ball to redirect it?

Action plan

Practise passing and ball control each week so that you increase your confidence in these aspects of play.

Chapter **8**

Individual practice drills for goalkeepers

THIS CHAPTER WILL:

- Help you to develop the skills and techniques required to become an effective goalkeeper.
- Provide drills and practices you can work on, either on your own or with a team-mate.

The previous chapter highlighted the basic skills of passing and ball control that all footballers need. However, goalkeeping is a specialized position, with specific skills and techniques that are unique in football. The role of the goalkeeper has changed over the years, so that they now need to be just as comfortable as outfield players with the ball at their feet. Balance and footwork are important, but obviously handling and catching ability are also essential skills. Look back at pages 20–21 in Chapter 1 to remind yourself of the key attributes of a good goalkeeper. Many of these technical skills, such as catching, diving, punching, kicking and throwing, can be improved with practice. This chapter provides some examples of drills and practices that you can try on your own or with a team-mate to improve your skills, as well as top advice on improving your game. Many of the practices need another person to 'deliver' the ball, but if you are able to use a wall then you can adapt the drills, using the wall to rebound the ball for you to catch or punch. If you are using a wall, please make sure it has a smooth finish, and that it is a safe area, not near to a road or windows.

Catching the ball

Catching is a basic skill that all goalkeepers should practise so that you can prepare for a catch automatically without thinking about it. Preparation is key – all movements should be made before the ball reaches your hands so that your hands are as still as possible when the catch is made. These top tips will help you become a 'safe hands' keeper:

For catches that are chest high or above:

- **Position your hands in the 'W' shape. The hands need to be placed together with outstretched thumbs, about 2 cm apart, forming a 'W' shape. The spacing is important – hands too close and the ball will bounce out, hands too far apart and the ball can slip through.**

- **Relax your hands but keep them strong so that they are prepared for impact – you are then more likely to grip the ball.**

- **Try not to move your hands towards the ball. Adjust your body position and get your hands ready in a position you judge best for the flight of the ball. Wait for the ball, keeping your hands steady, relaxed and still.**

For high catches position your hands in the 'W' shape.

For catches that are waist high or below:

- Position your hands so that they form a 'cup' shape with fingers slightly bent and pointing down and thumbs facing out.

- Bend your elbows and knees. Relax your hands but keep them strong so that they are prepared for impact.

- Lean slightly forward and when the ball reaches your hand bring your arms and hands in, to bring the ball safely into your chest.

For low catches position your hands so they form a cup shape.

Drills and skills

DRILL 1: QUICK HANDS

Purpose

To improve your basic handling and catching technique.

You will need:

1 football

2 cones

Activity

1 Use the cones to make a four-metre goal.

2 Stand in front of the goal and ask a team-mate to serve a ball on the volley towards the goal.

3 The server needs to be approximately ten metres away.

4 Catch the ball cleanly, using the 'cup' or 'W' shape techniques depending on the height of the serve.

Think about:

- Getting in your set position before each shot.

- Moving your body into line with the shot and letting the ball reach your hands – don't reach for the ball.

Target

Three sets of ten clean catches with a short rest after each set.

Progression

- Make the goal wider.
- Volley the ball with more pace.

Figure 8.1 **Drill 1: Quick hands**

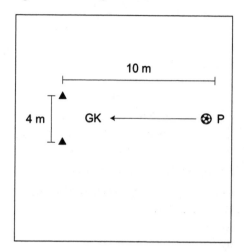
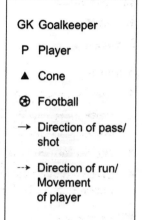

DRILL 2: TURN AND CATCH

Purpose

To practise reacting quickly to catch the ball.

You will need:

1 football

Activity

1   Ask a team-mate to stand with a ball approximately five metres away.

2   Face away from the player. They shout 'Turn!' and immediately volley or half-volley the ball towards you. You turn quickly to make the save.

3   Make sure the serve is strong enough to test you, but gives you time to turn and make the save.

4   Return the ball and turn away ready to repeat the drill.

Think about:

*   Getting your hands ready in the 'W' shape.
*   Turning quickly and getting both feet set and balanced to make the catch.

Target

Give yourself three sets of ten, with a short rest between each set.

Progression

- Vary the serve so it is not always straight at you. Shoot to either side, high and low.

Figure 8.2 **Drill 2: Turn and catch**

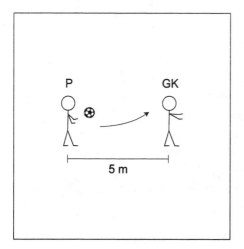

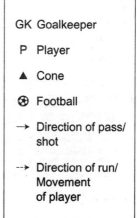

GK Goalkeeper

P   Player

▲   Cone

⊛   Football

→   Direction of pass/ shot

⇢   Direction of run/ Movement of player

DRILL 3: STOP THE BOUNCE

Purpose

To develop your technique in catching the ball.

You will need:

4 cones

2 footballs

Activity

1 Use the cones to make a ten-metre square grid.

2 Stand inside the grid.

3 Ask a team-mate to throw a ball up into the grid. Use quick movements to catch the ball before it touches the ground.

4 Once you have caught the ball, quickly roll it back to the player.

5 While the ball is rolling back, the player throws in the second ball to be caught. This is repeated, with the aim being to stop each ball touching the ground.

Think about:

- Getting into the 'set position' for each throw, with weight forward.

- Getting your hands ready, into the 'W' shape.

- Bringing the ball into the safety of your arms after each save.

Target

How many consecutive saves can you make in one minute?

Progression

- Vary the height of the delivery.
- Stand towards the front of the grid so the ball can be thrown over you.

Figure 8.3 **Drill 3: Stop the bounce**

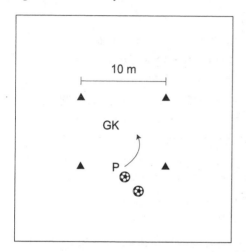

GK Goalkeeper

P Player

▲ Cone

⊕ Football

→ Direction of pass/ shot

--→ Direction of run/ Movement of player

DRILL 4: TWO-BALL PASSING

Purpose

To improve catching ability.

You will need:

2 footballs

Activity A

1　Face a team-mate, approximately three metres apart.

2　Have a ball each and throw them to each other at the same time, as you move sideways towards the right.

3　Pass the balls at about head/chest height and try to synchronize the throwing and catching.

4　After about 15 minutes, change direction and move sideways towards the left.

Activity B

1　Face a team-mate, approximately three metres apart. Have a ball each.

2　Your team-mate throws a ball to you and, at the same time, you throw your ball high into the air above your head. Catch the ball thrown to you and pass it back, then catch your own ball.

3　Try to synchronize the timing and repeat ten times.

Think about:

• Getting your hands into a 'W' shape.

• Concentrating and watching the ball you are about to catch.

Target

Count the number of consecutive catches. Aim to get a total of ten.

Progression

Increase the pace while maintaining the quality.

Figure 8.4 **Drill 4: Two-ball passing**

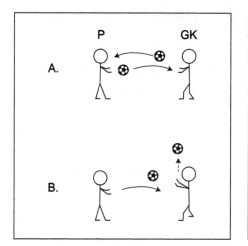
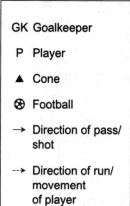

Shot stopping

Set position

When preparing for a shot coming directly at you, it is important that you are in a set position. The basic set position is your 'ready' stance, and you need to be in this position many times in a match. You should be relaxed but alert and ready to move quickly in any direction.

Practise moving into the following set position:

- feet shoulder width apart and facing forward
- knees slightly bent
- hands facing forward, about tummy height in front of the body
- fingers pointing downwards and thumbs on the outside
- body leaning slightly forward
- head still, eyes looking forward.

The correct set position

Before getting into this set position it is important that you have moved the correct distance from the goal line and at the correct angle from the near post to stop the shot. You need to move with short sideways movements to get into the correct starting place – which is usually a line drawn between the ball and the centre of the goal. This will depend on the position of the player with the ball, and the options that are available to that player. For example, if a player is about to take a long-range shot from 25 metres away, your first priority must be to position yourself not too far from the goal line to stop the ball going over your head into the goal. Then, after adopting the set position, you will have time to make a low save. If it is a high shot then you are in a position to recover and tip the ball over the bar. Just before any shot, it is ideal if your feet are still and equally balanced, with your bodyweight forward.

Top tip

Never put your weight on your heels as you may fall backwards when the shot is taken.

Quote | 'Being balanced when slightly out of position is better that being unbalanced but in the correct position. Therefore as the ball is being struck the goalkeeper must be set . . . this will give the goalkeeper the best opportunity to make a save.'

Martin Thomas, Assistant National
Goalkeeping Coach, The FA)

Drills and skills

DRILL 5: LOW SHOTS

Purpose

To practise moving into the 'set position' after each shot.

You will need:

1 football

2 cones

Activity

1   Make a three-metre goal with the cones and ask a team-mate to stand 20 metres away with a football.

2   Adopt the 'set position' ready for the player to take a low shot straight at you.

3   After you make the save, roll the ball back slightly to the side of the player so the angle changes.

4   Move to face the shot, adopting the 'set position' again.

5   Repeat for ten shots, all low and straight at you.

Think about:

* Getting your hands behind the ball.

* Getting your legs behind your hands in case the ball slips through.

* Your body shape for the 'set position'.

Target

Practise this until you automatically adopt the 'set position'.

Progression

* Vary the shot height, keeping the pace the same.

* Vary the shot pace, keeping the ball low.

* Vary both the shot height and pace so that you are unsure of the type of shot being faced.

Figure 8.5 **Drill 5: Low shots**

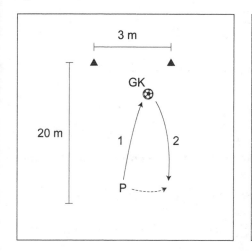

GK Goalkeeper

P Player

▲ Cone

⊕ Football

→ Direction of pass/
    shot

⇢ Direction of run/
    movement
    of player

DRILL 6: SHOT STOPPING

Purpose

To practise saving a variety of shots.

You will need:

1 football

4 cones

Activity

1   Use the cones to make two three-metre goals, about 20 metres apart.

2   Ask a team-mate to stand in front of one goal while you stand in the other.

3   The aim is to score past each other using a variety of strikes: volley, half-volley, or from the ground.

4   Use appropriate goalkeeping techniques for each shot: catching, diving and parrying when necessary.

Think about:

* Getting into the set position before each shot.

* Making a quick decision on the type of save, depending on the flight and pace of the ball.

* Concentrating on your kicking technique for the return.

Target

The first to score five goals is the winner.

Progression

* Bring the goals in a little so they are only 15 metres apart.

* Make the goals seven metres wide.

Figure 8.6 **Drill 6: Shot stopping**

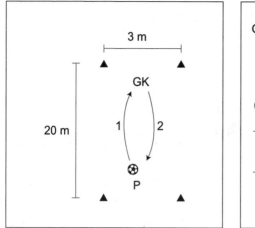

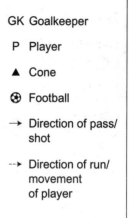

Narrowing the angle

You don't necessarily need to be great at maths to be a keeper, but it helps to know about angles. When you move forward off your goal line, you will be concerned with your left and right, the near post and the far post. You will also be concerned with the ball being kicked over your head. If you advance at an angle towards a player with the ball, or simply alter your position in the goal to stay in line with the ball, you must constantly position yourself so that you are in line with the ball and the goal. The further out the player is with the ball, the further you can venture off your line. The nearer the player with the ball is, the closer you must be to your goal line.

The first priority in angle play positioning is to protect the near post. The ball has a shorter distance to travel and its speed will be greater. This near post could be called the 'fast post' as the ball gets there quicker. You are trying to encourage the player to shoot to the far post as this is the 'slow post', giving you or your defenders more chance to make the save

Top tip

Try to position yourself so that you can get two hands to any ball struck to the near post, even if that means you can only get one hand on a ball struck to the far post.

Drills and skills

DRILL 7: HIGH AND LOW

Purpose

To practise saving angled shots.

You will need:

1 goal

1 football

Activity

1   Ask a team-mate to stand to one side of the penalty area at an angle to the goal. They give alternate throws or kicks, either high into the top corner or low just inside the post.

2   Stand in the correct place towards the near post to narrow the angle. Make sure you are in the set position.

3   Dive for the low throws and catch the high throws, then return the ball back to the server.

4   Quickly get back into the set position ready for the next throw.

Think about:

*   Getting into the set position before each throw.
*   Getting your angles correct so there is no gap at the near post.
*   Bringing the ball safely into your arms after each save.

Target

Make 20 saves before resting and repeating.

Progression

- Put more pace into the shots.
- Move to change the angles of shots.

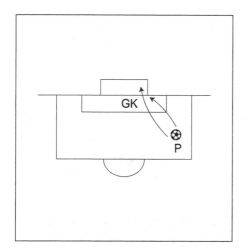

GK Goalkeeper

P Player

⊕ Football

→ Direction of pass/ shot

Reaction saves

A key attribute you need to develop as a goalkeeper is the ability to react quickly in different situations. This is particularly true for close-range shots, when you need to make instinctive saves with quick movements and quick hands.

Drills and skills

DRILL 8: DEFLECT AND REACT

Purpose

To speed up reactions for shot-stopping.

You will need:

6–8 cones (use spare shoes, if practising in you garden)

1 football

1 goal

Activity

1   Set up a number of cones in front of the goal, in the goal area.

2   Ask a team-mate to shoot from different angles along the ground, trying to hit the cones as a deflection.

3   You must try to react quickly to the deflected shots, either catching the ball or parrying it away.

4   Pass the ball back for the next shot.

Think about:

•   Watching the ball carefully, following its path.

•   Getting into the set position before each shot.

Target

Give yourself a score out of ten shots. Eight saves is excellent, anything over five is good.

Progression

•   Strike the shots with more pace.

•   Use two players to pass across to each other to change the angle before shooting.

Figure 8.8 **Drill 8: Deflect and react**

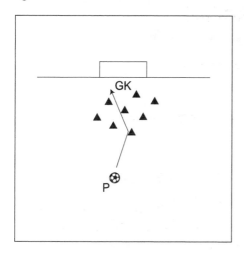

GK Goalkeeper

P Player

▲ Cone

⊕ Football

→ Direction of pass/
   shot

--→ Direction of run/
   Movement
   of player

Saves at close range need to be instinctive.

DRILL 9: OFF THE WALL

Purpose

To improve goalkeeper's reactions from shots.

You will need:

a wall

1 football

2 cones

Activity

1 Position two cones six metres apart facing a wall.

2 Stand at the near post, facing the wall.

3 A team-mate strikes the ball against the wall to go into the goal.

4 You react, either diving to save or moving across to catch or deflect the ball.

Think about:

- Getting into the set position.
- Following the flight of the ball as early as possible.
- Deciding quickly whether to catch, deflect, parry or block.

Target

Keep a score out of ten shots. Try to let in fewer than ten goals.

Progression

- Vary the service – volleys or half-volleys.
- Face the server so you need to turn and react.

Figure 8.9 **Drill 9: Off the wall**

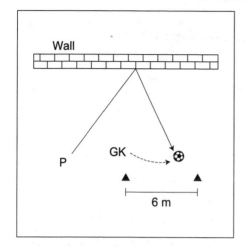

DRILL 10: JOG, CATCH AND DIVE

Purpose

To improve reactions when diving and catching.

You will need:

1 football

4 cones

Activity

1 Use the cones to make a ten-metre square area. Stand in the middle of the square.

2 Jog around the area, changing direction and speed as you jog.

3 Ask a team-mate to throw the ball to you, either rolling it along the ground for you to dive onto or throwing it into the air for you to catch.

4 Return the ball to the server, while continuing to jog.

Think about:

- Reacting quickly to the type of pass.
- Smothering the ball when diving, bringing it into your arms.
- Jumping for a high catch.

Target

Make 15 saves before resting and repeating.

Progression

- Make the throws more challenging – involving 'dummy' throws or throws further away from the keeper.

Figure 8.10 **Drill 10: Jog, catch and drive**

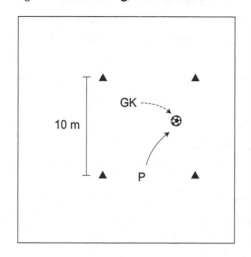

Only the keeper to beat

During a match there may be times when a striker is through on goal with only you to beat. Hopefully this doesn't happen too often – if it does, then some work is needed to improve your defence! In these 1 v 1 situations, it helps to be prepared and practised so that you make the task of scoring as difficult as possible for the striker.

Drills and skills

DRILL 11: 1 v 1 WITH KEEPER

Purpose

To practise goalkeeping against a striker running towards the goal with the ball.

You will need:

1 football

4 cones

Activity

1 Use the cones as corners of a ten-metre square grid.

2 Stand in the centre of the grid, facing a player with the ball.

3 The player attempts to dribble around you while staying in the grid.

4 The aim is for the striker to stop the ball under control in the area on the other side of the grid, or for you to save the ball or force it out of the grid.

5 This is repeated from both ends of the grid.

Think about:

• Delaying the attacker for as long as possible.

• Staying as big as possible, for as long as possible.

• Forcing the attacker wide if possible.

• Watching the ball, not the attacker's body movement.

• Leading with the hands, not with the feet if smothering or diving at feet.

Target

How many saves can you make out of ten 'attacks'?

Progression

*   The striker tries to score within four seconds. This encourages him/her to advance towards you at pace, which is far more realistic.

*   Rather than the attacker starting with the ball, you can start the practice by rolling the ball to the attacker, so that you can threaten their first touch.

Figure 8.11 **Drill 11: 1 v 1 with keeper**

GK Goalkeeper

P Player

▲ Cone

⊕ Football

→ Direction of pass/ shot

⇢ Direction of run/ Movement of player

DRILL 12: FIVE DIVES

Purpose

To practise diving onto a ball and improve fitness levels.

You will need:

5 footballs (or repeat with fewer balls)

1 goal and penalty area

Activity

1　Arrange the five balls in the area. Spread them out so they are well spaced.

2　Stand on the goal line. Run out and dive onto a ball. Pick it up and sprint back to the goal line, leaving the ball on the line.

3　Repeat this for each ball, until all five are on the goal line

4　If you have only one football, sprint out and dive as described above. Pick up the ball but instead of running back and placing the ball on the goal line, roll the ball out into a different position in the area. Now sprint back to the goal line before returning to dive on the ball. Repeat this until you have completed five dives.

Think about:

• Leading with your hands when diving on each ball.

• Recovering quickly, sprinting back to the line.

Target

Use a timer. Time your first attempt at five dives, rest and then try to beat your time.

Progression

If you want to work on fitness, put the balls further away and increase your pace.

Figure 8.12 **Drill 12: Five dives**

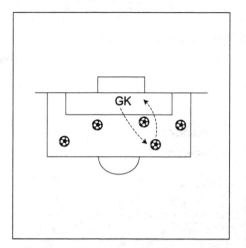

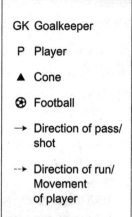

GK Goalkeeper

P Player

▲ Cone

⊕ Football

→ Direction of pass/
   shot

--→ Direction of run/
   Movement
   of player

Dealing with chip shots

When you face a chipped or high shot that goes over your head and could drop into the goal, it is important that you quickly use a 'recovery movement'. This isn't a backwards run or a full turn, but a sideward run. If the ball is going high over your left shoulder, take a quarter-turn to the left. Take the left foot back and cross over with your right leg, pushing off your right leg to gain height. Keep an eye on the ball and swing the right arm upward to flip the ball over the crossbar. To save a shot going over the other shoulder, the movements are a mirror image.

Drills and skills

DRILL 13: FLIP OVER

You will need:

a goal

several footballs

Purpose

To practise recovering backwards to flip a ball over the bar.

Activity

1 Stand in the goal area, in front of a goal on the edge of the six yard box.

2 Ask a player to chip the ball over the top of you from outside the penalty box. They aim to hit it high to drop just under the crossbar. This could be thrown if they find the delivery difficult.

3 Don't move until the ball has been kicked and then make a quick recovery movement to flip the shot over the bar.

4 Return to the start position before each shot.

Think about:

• Being ready and on your toes – quick footwork is needed.

• Getting the direction of the turn correct.

• Springing off the correct foot.

• Watching the ball and extending the correct arm to flip the ball over.

Target

How many saves can you make out of ten chips?

Progression

Start from further out from the goal line so that a sideward run is needed before a crossover and jump.

Figure 8.13 **Drill 13: Flip over**

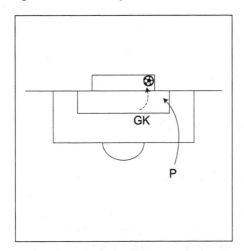

GK Goalkeeper

P   Player

▲   Cone

⊕   Football

→   Direction of pass/ shot

--→   Direction of run/ Movement of player

Diving

Diving technique

To be a top goalkeeper you need to enjoy diving on the ground for the ball. You may see outfield players diving spectacularly after they think they have been fouled, but not many of these players have the bravery or skill to dive at a striker's feet or throw themselves full length to deflect a ball around the post.

For sideways diving, the technique is important and varies for low shots along the ground and high shots.

Low shots

1   Hold the set position, staying relaxed but alert and keeping your eye on the ball.

2   You're aiming to stop the ball in front of you. If the shot is on your left, take a step towards the ball with your left foot, then spring and stretch out towards the ball to stop it as soon as possible.

3 Put your 'lower' hand behind the ball and the other hand on top.

4 Land on your hips, shoulder and side to spread the impact.

5 As you save the ball, bring the top leg in towards the ball. This stops you rolling onto your back.

6 Pull the ball safely into your arms towards your body.

High shots

1 Hold the set position, staying relaxed but alert and keeping your eye on the ball.

2 Take one or two steps sideways in the direction of the shot. The last step should be diagonally sideways and forwards and is the 'explosive step' providing the power to launch. If the shot is to your right, put weight down on your right leg, bending your knee and then springing up to your right.

3 As you launch from this step, swing the top knee (the left one in this example) up with your arms.

4 Catch the ball in the air.

5 Land on your upper arms, shoulders and hips to spread the impact.

6 As you land, roll sideways to a stop, pulling the ball safely into your arms towards your body.

Drills and skills

DRILL 14: OVER THE BALL

Purpose

To practise the correct technique for diving.

You will need:

2 footballs

Activity

1 Place a football on the ground to one side of you.

2 Ask a player to stand about three metres away and throw a ball to the far side of the ball on the ground. The ball that has been thrown should be at about knee height as it passes the ball on the ground.

3 Aim to dive directly over the ball on the ground without touching it, deflecting the ball that has been thrown or catching it in the air.

Think about:

• Pushing off a launch foot so that both feet are off the ground.

• Keeping your eye on the ball and deciding whether to parry or catch.

• Diving side on and landing on your shoulder and hip so the impact is spread.

Target

Dive five times in each direction, recording a score out of ten. Check your score to see if you are weaker in one direction. If so, increase the practice in the weak direction.

Progression

Throw the ball higher in the air to practise diving for high shots.

Figure 8.14 **Drill 14: Over the ball**

GK Goalkeeper

P Player

▲ Cone

⊕ Football

→ Direction of pass/
shot

⇢ Direction of run/
Movement
of player

DRILL 15: POST TO POST

Purpose

To improve the goalkeeper's diving technique.

You will need:

1 football

1 goal (or 2 cones/markers)

Activity

1　Stand in the centre of the goal, just off the line.

2　Ask a team-mate to stand about ten metres away and kick the ball towards one side of the goal, keeping the ball near the ground.

3　Dive to make the save, recover and roll the ball back to the server.

4　While the ball is rolling back, continue running to touch the post you dived towards.

5　Return to the centre and get yourself into the 'set position', ready for the next shot.

Think about:

- Recovering quickly after the dive.
- Getting into the 'set position' before each shot.
- Bringing the ball into your arms after each save.

Target

Make ten continuous saves, then rest before repeating.

Progression

Increase the pace of delivery.

Figure 8.15 **Drill 15: Post to post**

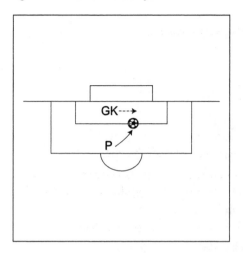

GK Goalkeeper

P   Player

▲   Cone

⊗   Football

→   Direction of pass/
    shot

⇢   Direction of run/
    Movement
    of player

DRILL 16: QUICK DIVES

Purpose

To practise diving for low shots.

You will need:

1 football

Activity

1 Stand approximately five metres away from a team-mate.

2 Pass the ball between you – take one or two touches and pass the ball firmly.

4 After four to six passes like this, your team-mate puts a pass to one side of you with a little more pace, shouting 'Dive!' at the same time.

4 You need to react quickly, diving down to stop the ball with your hands.

5 Recover quickly, getting up and continuing the passing.

Think about:

- Making solid 'push passes' with the side of your foot.
- 'Collapsing' quickly to dive on the ball.
- Bringing the ball safely into your arms before standing up.

Target

Make five successful saves before resting.

Progression

- Play just one touch passing.

Figure 8.16 **Drill 16: Quick dives**

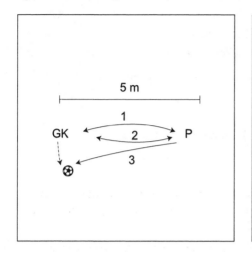

GK Goalkeeper

P Player

▲ Cone

⊗ Football

→ Direction of pass/ shot

--→ Direction of run/ Movement of player

Deflecting the ball

There are times when it is not possible to catch a ball when diving to your left or right because you are fully extended and can only reach the ball with one hand. You need to practise deflecting or parrying the ball around the post, keeping your hands strong enough to change the direction of the ball.

Drills and skills

DRILL 17: PARRYING SHOTS

Purpose

To practise diving low to parry the ball away from the goal.

You will need:

6 footballs

4 cones

Activity

1 Find an area of soft grass or sand.

2 Set up two pairs of cones as small 'goals', about three metres apart. Imagine the real goal is between these and the inside cones are level with the goalposts.

3 Position yourself between the two sets of cones. A player passes the ball along the ground, aiming for each small goal with alternate passes. The pass or shot is important. Make sure it pushes you to make an extended dive.

4 Slide or dive along the surface, extending yourself and aiming to deflect the ball on the outside of the cones.

Think about:

• Recovering quickly after each dive, standing up and getting balanced before diving to the other side.

• Keeping your knees flexed, and staying relatively low to the ground.

- Keeping a stiff wrist to prevent the power of the shot from bending back the arm.

- Picturing your body shape as you dive. Could you use two hands? What are your legs doing?

Target

How many consecutive saves can you make?

Progression

- Speed up the practice and pass the ball with more pace.

- Make the direction of shots or passes random.

Figure 8.17 **Drill 17: Parrying shots**

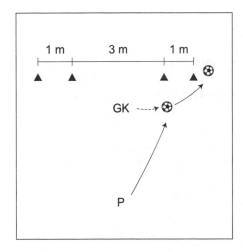
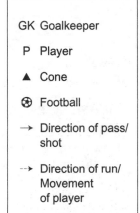

Dealing with crosses

One of the greatest difficulties for most goalkeepers is dealing with crosses. Many keepers favour crosses from one side, with problems in punching or catching from the other side. Others find the decision-making difficult:

- Do I move out to try to catch this?
- Should I punch or catch?
- Shall I leave this for the defence to clear and stay on my line?
- Should I go front post or back post?

These problems often relate to the starting position of the keeper, when there are difficulties moving to the near post or far post areas. The starting point is dependent on the position of the player crossing the ball. Remember these key points:

- Turn to face the player making the cross. If the player is quite close then fully face him/her. If the player is further away, near the touchline, then you can make a quarter turn towards the goal area. This is a more 'open' position so that you can watch the cross and the players in the area.

- If the ball is out on the wing, position yourself about midway between the posts, so that you are confident that you can cover the near and far posts. If the player crossing the ball is closer to goal, then your priority is to defend the near post, so move forward, towards this post.

- If it is a near-post or central cross make a quick and decisive movement towards the ball, watching it all the way. If it is very crowded it may be safer to punch the ball. If possible, catch the ball and bring it safely into your arms.

- If it is a far-post cross, use the 'recovery movement', making a quarter turn and a cross-over step. Keep your eye on the ball and, if it is not possible to catch it, flip or punch the ball away or over the bar.

Key factors to think about when dealing with crosses:

- Sort out your starting position and stance.
- Assess the flight of the ball.
- Communicate loudly and clearly, shouting, 'Keeper!'
- Approach the ball by the shortest route.
- Take off from your favoured foot.
- Catch or punch the ball at the highest and safest point.
- Land safely.

Drills and skills

DRILL 18: FOUR GOAL CROSSING

Purpose

To practise dealing with crosses from the left and right side of the goal.

You will need:

1 football

8 cones (or other markers)

Activity

1   Use the cones to set up four six-metre goals inside the penalty area.

2   Ask a team-mate (preferably a goalkeeper) to stand on one side of the area, while you stand in one of the goals on the other side of the area.

3   Cross the ball to each other to catch. Crosses can be from opposite goals or from a more acute angle.

4   Move into either goal on your side so you can receive crosses from your right and left.

Think about:

*   Sorting out your starting position, facing the ball being crossed to you.
*   Watching the flight of the ball.
*   Shouting 'Keeper!' as you move to the ball.
*   Jumping high and landing safely.

Target

Take three sets of ten crosses. Rest after each set. Assess your performance: Which side do you prefer? How do your near-post catches compare with your far-post saves?

Progression

Include another player in the area to put yourself under pressure for each cross.

Figure 8.18 **Drill 18: Four goal crossing**

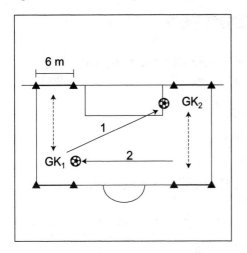

Punching to clear

Punching the ball is a very good option if catching is too risky in a crowded penalty area. If you watch Pepe Reina, goalkeeper for Liverpool FC, warm up before a match, he spends a long time with the coach practising his punches. He tries to redirect the ball high, far and wide out of the penalty area. This is what you should aim for with any punch: can you make the ball fly high, far and wide? Never punch downwards and, if possible, try to get both fists to the ball. Fold the fingers and press the knuckles together so that the thumbs are together and facing upwards towards you. Try to get to the ball at a point in its flight so that it is higher than an opponent could reach with their head.

Dominating the box

Most top goalkeepers like to dominate their penalty area or, for crosses, at least the small box in the penalty area. They like to be in a position where they can be first to the ball when possible, enabling them to intercept or stop any potentially dangerous situation. They dominate vocally as well, sorting the defence out and making sure both teams know who is 'bossing' the area.

These dominant keepers are not just physically commanding their box, but psychologically. The defenders will be confident that the box belongs to the keeper, and it also affects the opposition. A goalkeeper who dominates the box can cause teams to cross less, or cross to the top of the area. The through pass also becomes less effective and teams are likely look to push the ball wide instead.

To dominate the box, the goalkeeper must:

- be courageous
- be quick-thinking to anticipate the pass
- have quick reactions
- make good decisions
- be physically alert, starting a movement as, or before, the ball is passed.

Drills and skills

DRILL 19: DOMINATING THE BOX

Purpose

To practise catching crosses into the box from different angles.

You will need:

1 football

4 cones

Activity

1 Use the cones to make a 15-metre square grid.

2 Stand in the grid.

3 Your team-mate crosses the ball into the box from a position 15–20 metres outside the box for you to catch or punch.

4 Vary the crosses so that they are from different starting points and different heights.

5 Make decisions about whether to catch or punch.

Think about:

- Assessing the speed, height and angle of the ball.
- Being ready to make quick changes of direction.
- Making a decision whether to catch or punch.
- Using your full height to catch or punch the ball.
- Dominating the box!

Target

Count the consecutive clean catches you make. When punching, try to punch the ball out of the box.

Progression

Practise with other players in the box, sometimes with no pressure but just a congested area, sometimes with challenges for the ball.

Figure 8.19 **Drill 19: Dominating the box**

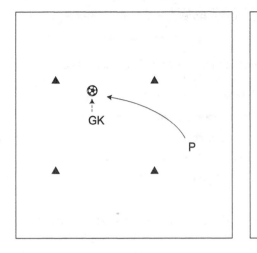

GK Goalkeeper

P Player

▲ Cone

⊕ Football

→ Direction of pass/shot

⇢ Direction of run/Movement of player

Distribution with feet

Goalkeepers are now expected to be as comfortable as outfield players with the ball at their feet. As well as goal kicks, drop kicks and punts, you need to deal with back passes and the ball running through to you to be cleared with your feet. It helps to be able to use both feet (not always easy!) and have a range of techniques to use, depending on the pass needed. Chapter 7 outlined the basic passing skills you need to practise:

- **the push pass for short distances**
- **the low driven pass for more distance**
- **the lofted pass to 'wedge' the ball above head height.**

Goal kicks

It is always best if you can take the goal kicks rather than an outfield player. This increases the number of players you can pass to and pushes play up the pitch. With an outfield player taking the goal kick, a striker could wait on the edge of the area and not be in an off-side position. Here are some technique reminders when taking a goal kick:

- **Place your standing leg beside and slightly behind the ball.**
- **Swing your kicking leg forward and 'through' the ball.**
- **Add an explosive 'punch' to your kick to generate distance.**
- **Keep your eye on the ball all the time.**

Top tip

Aim for either wing when taking a goal kick. If you kick down the centre, there is more chance of the opposition's midfield and defence clearing the ball back into your half. Also, a poor kick in front of goal could put you under immediate pressure.

Drop kicks

The drop kick is a difficult skill to master, but it can be a very quick and accurate way of passing a ball to a team-mate. The technique involves dropping the ball from one hand in front of you and slightly to one side of your kicking leg. You kick the ball just after it touches the ground – a half-volley. Short low passes can be made with a 'punching' kick with little follow-through. The more you swing through with your leg the further and higher the kick, but also the less likely it is that you will be accurate. Practise this yourself, trying short drop kicks and then longer passes. How accurate are you with your kicks?

Statistics

In research of goalkeeper distribution in Youth Academy matches, it was found that short passes from the goalkeeper were 100 per cent successful in reaching a team-mate. Long passes were less successful, with only 40 per cent of passes kept in possession.

The volley

This is basically a volley from your hands. The technique is similar to the drop kick but you kick the ball before it touches the ground. The throw up is important, placing the ball slightly forward and to one side of your kicking leg so that it drops nicely for your foot to meet the ball as it swings through. Once again, the shorter passes are easier to control. If you try for distance there is a good chance the ball will 'slice' off your foot, spinning to one side and dropping short. If you are not confident at volleying, concentrate on using it for shorter passes to either wing. Practise the technique until you have the confidence to use the volley for both long and short passes.

Drills and skills

DRILL 20: PASSING WITH YOUR FEET

Purpose

To practise short and medium passes with both feet.

You will need:

1 football

Activity

Work with a team-mate to practise a range of passes.

A For short passes stand 10–20 metres apart. Use the push pass.

1 With one touch, use only the right foot. Pass the ball ten times.

2 Still with one touch, use only the left foot. Pass the ball ten times.

3 Continue with one touch but use alternate feet – right, left, right . . . Pass the ball ten times.

B For medium passes stand 20–40 metres apart.

1 Use two touches to receive the ball and pass to your team-mate.

2 Use the three basic passing techniques in turn – push pass, low drive and lofted pass – to return the ball.

Think about:

• Making a good first touch.

• Keeping your eye on the ball at all times.

• Practising each technique until you automatically prepare for and carry out a particular passing skill.

Target

Take ten passes and try to limit the poor passes to just one out of ten.

Progression

Vary the delivery so that your team-mate passes the ball along the ground and in the air for you to control and return.

Figure 8.20 **Drill 20: Passing with your feet**

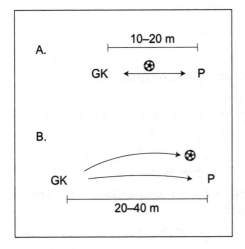

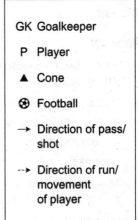

DRILL 21: FIND YOUR RANGE

Purpose

To improve long-range kicking techniques.

You will need:

1 football

8 cones (or other markers)

Activity

1 Set up two five-metre squares with the cones, approximately 40 metres apart.

2 You stand in one square and a team-mate stands in the other.

3 Take goal kicks to each other, aiming to loft the ball using a wedge technique.

4 Score a point for each kick that lands in the square.

5 Use the same activity to practise volleying or half-volleying the ball as a punt or drop kick.

Think about:

• Keeping your eye on the ball as you strike it.

• Placing your standing leg in the correct position, to the side and slightly behind the ball.

• Following through with a 'punch' of your leg to generate speed.

Target

First to reach five points is the winner. Play three games each for goal kicks, volleys and half-volleys.

Progression

• Increase the distance of the passes.

Figure 8.21 **Drill 21: Find your range**

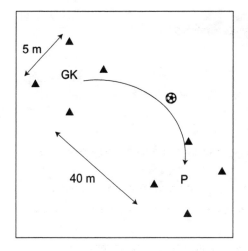

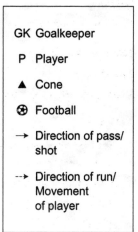

GK Goalkeeper

P Player

▲ Cone

⊕ Football

→ Direction of pass/shot

--→ Direction of run/Movement of player

Distribution with hands

Goalkeepers pass using their hands as often as a kicked pass or clearance during a match. A throw can be a more accurate pass and can also be quicker to set a counter-attack going. There are several different types of throw, but the main ones are the underarm and overarm throws.

Underarm throw

This is a useful throw to an unmarked team mate within a 10–30 metre range. It is very accurate when delivered properly, as an underarm bowl. The key is to throw it in response to the movements of the receiving player. The receiving player should make a run or turn to indicate the direction and pace of the ball they would like to receive. Only roll the ball out if a player is ready for it, and at a pace that is comfortable for the player.

Underarm throw

Top tip

It can be risky to roll a ball out to a player in front of the goal. Always look wide – this type of pass can be used to reach a wide player but often needs a bit of pace to reach them.

Overarm throw

This is the most usual type of throw made by keepers. It has the advantage of distance and pace and it can be used to throw the ball over the heads of the opposition forwards. Hold the ball with both hands and take it backward in the palm and fingers of the throwing hand until this arm is straight (the other hand releases as the ball goes back). Swing the arm upward and forward, releasing the ball from the tip of the fingers.

Overarm throw

Top tip

Practise putting spin on the ball by chopping down with the little finger as you release it. This gives a bit more pace and makes the ball 'curve' off the first bounce into the stride path of the receiving player.

Choosing the best distribution

The main aim you should have when kicking or throwing a ball out is for your team to keep possession. This could be as a quick counter-attack, or it could be a short pass to start a move off in your half. Obviously you need to be accurate and pass with the correct pace, but whichever method of passing the ball you choose it will have a great effect on the way your team attacks. Once you have picked the ball up or caught it, you have six seconds to make a pass or put it on the ground to play it to another player. Sometimes you will want to use this time to slow down play and allow your team-mates to get into more attacking positions. At other times you will want to pass quickly to catch the opposition out with a counter-attack. On the whole, short passes have more chance of success, either by hand or foot, but an accurate long kick or throw can be a powerful weapon.

Statistics

In research of goalkeeper distribution in Youth Academy matches, it was found that underarm throws were 100 per cent successful in reaching a player and overarm throws were 80 per cent successful. This compared with a lower success rate for kicking, with 25 per cent of long goal kicks and 35 per cent of drop kick passes successfully reaching a team-mate.

The statistics above show the strength of throwing the ball to a team-mate – there is a very good chance the player will have possession of the ball from your pass. In the same research, it was found that 95 per cent of all short distributions from the goalkeeper (including those made with feet) successfully reached a player, compared with 39 per cent of long distributions. This has implications for you as a goalkeeper:

- **if you want your team to retain possession you should look to distribute the ball over short distances whenever possible.**
- **Short passes have more chance of success with underarm and overarm throws, as well as passes with your feet.**

Drills and skills

DRILL 22: WALL THROWS

Purpose

To practise different throwing techniques.

You will need:

a wall

1 football

Activity

1   Stand about two metres in front of a wall with a ball in your hand.

2   Throw the ball at the wall, using underarm throws so that it rebounds back to you.

3   Repeat ten times so that you can concentrate on the technique.

4   Move on to overarm throws – stand further back for this type of throw.

Think about:

*   Accuracy – aim for a particular spot on the wall.
*   Perfecting your technique – picture your arm, head, leg and body movements for each throw.

Target

Take ten throws at a spot on the wall. What is your score out of ten?

Progression

Try putting more pace and, possibly, spin into your overarm throw to get more distance.

Figure 8.22 **Drill 22: Wall throws**

GK Goalkeeper

P　Player

▲　Cone

⊛　Football

→　Direction of pass/ shot

-→　Direction of run/ movement of player

DRILL 23: OVERARM ACCURACY

Purpose

To practise accurate distribution by throwing.

You will need:

1 football

3 cones/ markers

Activity

1　Set up the three cones in a line about five metres apart.

2　Ask a team-mate to stand behind the cones while you stand with the ball about 20 metres away.

3　Your team-mate runs behind one of the cones and you must throw an accurate overarm pass at that particular cone.

4   Continue this with your team-mate deciding which cone to
      stand behind and returning the ball after each throw.

Think about:

*   Being in the set position ready for the return pass.
*   Using the correct technique with a straight arm and releasing
    the ball from the tip of your fingers.

Target

Take three throws at each cone. How many can you hit?

Progression

*   Stand further back for a longer throw.
*   Put spin on the ball so it turns in towards the cone.

Figure 8.23 **Drill 23: Overarm accuracy**

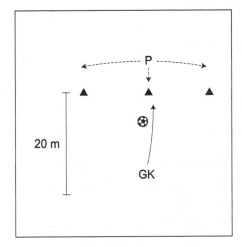

Summary

- When catching a ball, preparation is vital. Get your hands ready into a 'W' shape for high catches or a 'cup' shape for low catches.

- Getting into the 'set position' is essential before attempting to save any shot.

- Diving technique varies for high shots and low shots, but both involve landing on your upper arms, shoulders and hips to spread the impact.

- Sort out your starting position and stance when dealing with crosses.

- Short passes with hands or feet are more successful than long passes if you want to keep possession.

Self-tester

- What is the 'W' shape?
- Describe the 'set position' and demonstrate it.
- Which post is the most important for you to cover for a shot from a narrow angle – the near post (nearest the ball) or far post?

Action Plan

Plan a six-week training programme for yourself based around the six areas highlighted in this chapter:

- catching
- shot stopping
- diving

- dealing with crosses
- distribution with feet
- distribution with hands.

Focus on each area for a week, reading the tips on techniques and choosing some of the drills to practise the skills.

References

'Goalkeeping Development: Dealing with 1 v 1 when the attacker is through on goal', Martin Thomas, Assistant National Goalkeeping Coach, The Football Association (*FA Insight 2001*, Volume 5, Issue 1)

'Reactions: Principles and Practices', Martin Thomas, Assistant National Goalkeeping Coach, The Football Association (*FA Insight 2004*, Volume 7, Issue 2)

'Analysis of Goalkeepers' Distribution in Youth Academy Football', James Morton and Michael Court (*FA Insight 2002*, Volume 5, Issue 3)

Chapter 9

Tactics and teamwork

THIS CHAPTER WILL:
- Highlight some tactics and support play that will help you to become an effective goalkeeper within a team.
- Provide coaching tips for key goalkeeping tactics needed during a match, both in possession and out of possession.

The goalkeeper as a sweeper

One of the most difficult decisions you will have as a keeper is whether to advance off your line or out of the area to sweep up balls played behind the defence. Your timing needs to be good. Any hesitation can give a striker a chance to beat you to the ball, and you may be in danger of fouling the striker or allowing them a simple chance on goal. Alternatively, if you come too far off your line you may be in danger of being lobbed.

Your starting position in relation to the ball should be approximately on a line between the ball and the centre of the goal. If the ball is in the attacking third of the pitch towards the opponents' goal, then you should be positioned in an advanced position, approximately on the edge of your area. Make sure you are on your front foot in anticipation of a ball being played over the top of the defence. This is obviously only a guideline, as there are a number of factors that can alter your decision of how far to advance. These include:

• playing conditions
• player with the ball
• the depth of the defenders
• the position of the defenders.

Playing conditions

Playing with the wind or against the wind will cause you problems, as will playing in wet conditions. The ball played behind the defence will skid through to you, whereas in muddy conditions the ball is likely to hold up.

Player with the ball

The player in possession of the ball should determine your starting position. For example, if the ball is around the halfway line, the questions you need to ask yourself are:

• **Is there a chance of the player in possession playing the ball over me into the goal? If that player is David Beckham then the answer is yes, whereas other players may not be able to do it.**
• **Is there pressure on the ball? If there is no pressure then the player could pass the ball behind the defence.**
• **Can the player consistently play accurate balls in behind the defence with a variety of techniques? If you were facing a player such as Steven Gerrard you would need to be wary of his passing skills.**

The depth of the defenders

The depth of the defenders will determine how far you need to 'sweep' up behind the defence. Teams that defend very high up the pitch and play the offside trap need to have a goalkeeper with good pace and anticipation who is willing to take up advanced starting positions.

The position of the defenders

The position of the defenders who are marking the attackers will determine your starting position. If there is no pressure on the ball and the defender is marking too tight, there is a chance the ball may be played over the top of the defence, so you need to be in an advanced position to sweep up and clear the danger. If the defender is marking correctly, by dropping off the attacker, then you can drop back, as any ball now played behind the defence should be dealt with by the defender. You can then give the defender the option of playing the ball back to you to relieve the pressure.

Setting walls for free kicks

The goalkeeper must organize the defence in a free kick.

Quote | 'The goalkeeper must decide how many players should be in the wall and which side to position the wall.'

Micky Adams

Nearly one-third of goals are scored from set plays, which shows the importance of being organized defensively. If a free kick is awarded to the opposition on the edge of the area, then the defending team must move quickly and positively to support you in goal. Your role is crucial. You must organize the defence quickly and your instructions need to be clear, concise and loud. These are the types of questions you need to ask yourself:

- **Is the free kick direct or indirect?**
- **Where is the ball – can you judge the angle and distance?**
- **How many and which players are needed in the wall?**
- **Where should the tallest players go?**
- **Is the wall in the correct position for you?**
- **Do you want players charging the ball?**
- **Where is your starting position?**
- **What are the positions of the players not in the wall? Are they marking players or zones?**

Use the order shown in Figure 9.1 to set a wall for a free kick at either side of the penalty area. If the free kick is directly in front of goal then the wall should be more central, for example:

1. **The first player (A) in the wall is an important 'marker'. He/she needs to take a line between the ball and the near post, nine metres from the ball.**
2. **Decide on the number of players in the wall. They join the first player to cover one side of the goal.**

Figure 9.1 **Wall set up for a free kick at either side of the penalty area**

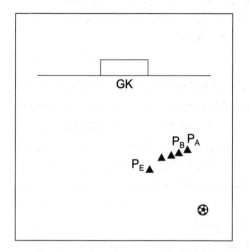

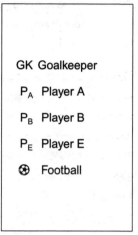

3. Once lined up, they take one pace to the right or left (depending on side of kick) to stop the ball curling around the outside of the wall into the near post. Player B is now in line with the near post.

4. One player (E) can stand in line with the far post, ready to charge the ball as soon as it is touched.

5. Your position as goalkeeper needs to be just off-centre of the goal and just in front of the goal line so that you can make an effort to save the ball on either side of the goal. Try to have a full view of the ball.

6. Wait until the ball is struck before making your first movement.

When you watch matches, either live or on television, study the goalkeeper when a free kick is given in a shooting position. He/she usually moves very quickly to the near post to line up one of the players with the ball, before moving back to the centre of goal. They are very vocal, shouting instructions and giving hand signals to show the number of players in the wall and the position they want. Watch their movements and learn from them – they will have practised free kicks for hours on the training ground.

Quote | 'The success I have at free kicks is five per cent skill and 95 per cent successful imagery.'
Gianfranco Zola

Imagery is a powerful tool used by all top players, including goalkeepers. Imagery, visualization, mental rehearsal and mental practice are all common terms used to describe the process of using your imagination to see yourself performing, say, a save from a free kick. If you are able to use all your senses to create an action in your mind before actually carrying out the activity, research has shown that there is more chance of success. This is also true for imagining a positive outcome to a match. If you think and see yourself performing well, you will generally perform well. Try using imagery yourself in different situations:

- **before going to sleep at night**
- **pre-match**
- **during training**
- **during a break in matches**
- **just before you are about to face a corner, free kick or penalty.**

Facing penalties

A goalkeeper can use one of three strategies when facing a penalty kick:

- **guess in advance which side the ball is likely to go and then stick with this decision**
- **wait until the penalty taker strikes the ball and then react based on the ball's early flight path**
- **anticipate where the ball is likely to go based on the penalty taker's run-up and body shape.**

Although you may prefer to dive to one side of the goal or the other, a strategy of moving in the preferred direction or 'guessing' is based purely on chance with a low probability of success.

The 'wait and react' strategy may work, particularly if the penalty is poorly struck and close to the middle of the goal. However, if it is a good penalty, requiring you to dive towards the corner of the goal, reacting to the ball is unlikely to be successful.

Research shows that the average time for the ball to travel from the penalty spot to the goal line is 500 milliseconds (half a second), whereas goalkeepers' reaction and movement times average around 550 milliseconds. To have a reasonable chance of success, goalkeepers must begin to move just before the moment the penalty-taker strikes the ball. This means that a goalkeeper needs to look at the penalty taker's run up and body shape before the kick to have more chance of a successful penalty save.

So what information should a goalkeeper look for when a player is running up and taking a penalty? In past research, the kicking leg has been shown as an area for the keeper to focus on, whereas more recent research has shown the importance of the non-kicking leg (Ian Franks, 1999). Franks argued that the non-kicking foot is positioned so that it points towards the ball's likely direction, while others argue that the angle of the foot during the downswing shows the likely direction of the ball.

There are no definite answers – otherwise more penalties would be saved in matches! However, there are other clues to look out for: players may look in the direction they want the ball to go, or the run-up could make it very obvious which direction the ball will be heading. Just remember to watch the player carefully as the kick is about to be taken. Make sure you are light on your feet, moving on the spot so you are

ready to leap into action. Make yourself 'look big'. Always remember that the penalty taker will be a lot more nervous than you are, so do everything you can to make the player as nervous as possible. They are expected to score, but saving a penalty is a great way of becoming a hero and changing a game!

Top tip

When you see a penalty being taken on television or at a match, try to predict the side of the goal the player will kick towards. On replays, does the body shape or run-up give any information away about the direction?

Counter-attacking – the goalkeeper's role

Goalkeeping is the first line of the attack as well as the last line of defence. Goalkeepers have great control over the pace and type of attack for a team. When counter-attacking as a team, you are trying to attack the opposition as quickly as possible after winning possession of the ball. This is when the opposition is likely to be disorganized and more vulnerable. A good counter-attack can start from the goalkeeper. If you are in possession of the ball there are a number of decisions that you need to make before starting a quick attack. Your 'vision' determines where the opposition can be exploited. Try to:

- decide whether to run with the ball or distribute early from where the catch was made
- look at the runs of team-mates and select the best option
- choose the correct technique to distribute the ball to that particular area, possibly a javelin/overarm throw or a drop kick or punt (half-volley/volley)
- decide whether the ball needs to be distributed to feet or space
- make sure the quality of the distribution is good in terms of timing, weight and accuracy
- think about the height of the distribution – does it need to clear opposing players?
- make sure that the defensive shape of the team is correct in case the attack breaks down.

The back-pass law

As a goalkeeper, you are obviously the only player in your team who can handle the ball while it is in play. However, there are times when you are not allowed to handle the ball inside the area.

Here is part of Law 12 from FIFA's 'Laws of the Game', relating to goalkeepers:

An indirect free kick is awarded to the opposing team if a goalkeeper, inside his own penalty area, commits any of the following five offences:

- **takes more than six seconds while controlling the ball with his hands before releasing it from his possession**
- **touches the ball again with his hands after it has been released from his possession and has not touched any other player**
- **touches the ball with his hands after it has been deliberately kicked to him by a team-mate**
- **touches the ball with his hands after he has received it directly from a throw-in taken by a team-mate**

Subject to the terms of Law 12, a player may pass the ball to his own goalkeeper using his head or chest or knee, etc. If, however, in the opinion of the referee, a player uses a deliberate trick while the ball is in play in order to circumvent the Law, the player is guilty of unsporting behaviour. He is cautioned, shown the yellow card and an indirect free kick is awarded to the opposing team from the place where the infringement occurred.

So, if a team-mate intentionally passes the ball back to you, you cannot handle the ball with your hands. You must use your feet or head to control or clear the ball. Indirect kicks are awarded at the spot where the ball is handled. However, if the referee interprets that there was no actual intent to pass the ball back then no indirect kick is awarded. The ball may be passed back using the head, chest or knee. However, if a trick or flick is used, for example, to lift the ball from the feet to the chest, that is considered unsporting behaviour and an indirect kick is awarded.

During a match, you need to think quickly and make decisions about picking the ball up or kicking it clear after a back pass. This has altered the way goalkeepers play the game, as you now need to be a better all-round footballer. You need to be able to control the ball with your feet, run or move with the ball and pass accurately. The greatest problems are caused when goalkeepers need to clear the ball with their first touch, while under pressure from an opposing striker. It is essential that you are a confident kicker of the ball, for your own sake, and also so that team-mates have confidence in you.

You need to work together with out-field players in training so that they are clear about the best ways of passing back to you. Players need to think before passing:

- Is passing to the keeper the best option?
- Where are the opposing players?
- Where is the keeper?
- Has the keeper called for the ball?
- Which foot do I pass to?
- At what speed do I need to pass the ball?

This is a lot to think about, and you can help the player make the correct decision by asking yourself:

- Can I get into a good position for a pass?
- Have I communicated with the player?
- Do I want a pass or will it be better to clear it away?
- Does the player know which foot I prefer to kick with?
- Where are the attacking players?
- Are there any players that I can pass to?

When the ball is passed back to you, the best option is to maintain possession whenever possible. If you have time, take a touch to control the ball and pass it to one of your players. You need to be absolutely sure that there are no attackers nearby, but don't look up to check for danger as the ball is reaching your feet in case you miss the ball. Be aware of player positions *before* the ball is passed and keep your eyes on the ball as you control or kick it. When in doubt, clear the ball away from danger with distance, height and width.

Summary

- Decision-making is vital as a goalkeeper, particularly when deciding whether to come out as a 'sweeper' to stop an attack.

- The goalkeeper needs to be in control of the setting of a wall for any free kick around his or her penalty area.

- To increase the chance of saving a penalty, move as the player is about to kick and watch their run up, feet and body shape to decide on the direction the ball will travel.

- The back-pass law has made ball control and passing with the feet an important skill for goalkeepers.

Self-tester

- The ball is played through your defence towards the penalty area. Give three factors that could affect your decision on how far to come out for the ball.

- You are lining up a wall for a free kick on the corner of the penalty box. Where are you likely to line up the first player in the wall?

- One of your players flicks a ball up with his feet onto his head and nods it back to you in goal. The referee awards an indirect free kick to the other team. Is this correct or incorrect?

Action plan

Discuss these tactics and ideas with your coach. Ask to practise some of them during training sessions with the other players so that you have increased confidence in different situations during a match.

References

The 'Supporting Role of the Goalkeeper', Martin Thomas, Assistant National Goalkeeping Coach, The Football Association (*FA Insight 2000*, Vol 3, Issue 3)

'The Goalkeeper's Role within the Counter Attacking Strategy', Martin Thomas, Assistant Goalkeeping Coach, The Football Association (*FA Insight 2000*, Vol 4, issue 1)

'Goalkeeping: Organization of Defensive walls around the penalty box', Martin Thomas, Assistant National Goalkeeping Coach, The Football Association (*FA Insight 1999*, Vol 2, Issue 3)

'Preparing Goalkeepers for Success at Penalty Kicks: A Sports Science Perspective', Mark Williams, Paul Ward, Geert Savelsbergh and John Van Der Kamp (*FA Insight 2001*, Volume 4, Issue 4)

Part 4

Developing your game

Chapter 10

Parents, coaches and clubs

THIS CHAPTER WILL:
- Help you to understand how important parents or carers are to your development as a player.
- Explain the roles played by the coach and parent.
- Show how you can work successfully with your coach.
- Provide guidance on choosing a club.

Parent power

One of the biggest influences on your football interest and involvement will be your parents or carers. Your coach or a teacher at school may fine-tune your dribbling skills and improve your passing techniques, but your parents will have the major impact on your desire, attitudes, values and ambitions.

Research has shown that the interest and support of parents is vital to a young player's participation in sport. It has, however, also shown that much of the pressure and anxiety that young players feel in sport comes from their parents. You need to be aware of this; some of the influence of your parents on your football experience will be positive and constructive, but some will not.

Positive and negative effects

Most parents have the best intentions in mind when they support and help their child to become footballers, whether for the local park team or for a professional club. However, these good intentions can sometimes lose their way as parents get involved with the emotional roller-coaster ride of junior football. We have all witnessed the parents who shout and scream from the touchline, following every movement of their own child, with no awareness of the other players in the team. Goals, results and their child's involvement in the game are all-important, with criticism as likely as encouragement when talking to their child following a game.

These types of parents believe that they are supporting their eight-year-old, but instead they may be building up possible problems for them. They probably mean well – they just want their son or daughter to succeed, but they just get too animated and involved. So why does this happen?

Parents have a strong desire to 'make things right' for their son or daughter, which can be taken too far, however well intentioned. A belief that there is a right and a wrong way to do things can lead to confrontation, for example, by telling a child what he or she should have done, rather than respecting them and encouraging the child to work things out for themselves.

Many parents are reliving their sporting experience through their child, which is one reason why they want as many opportunities open to their child as possible. If their son or daughter fails, it is a reflection of their own sporting ability, or inability, and it is felt acutely. Once again, the intentions of trying to maximize opportunities are good but the effect when seen to be a failure can be negative. The pressure on a player of losing or playing badly can be doubled if their parent reacts in a frustrated and angry way.

It is not easy to be a good parent of a competitive football player. As a player you need to be aware of this, and encourage parents to:

- be supportive without telling you how to do or not do something (unless you ask for help)
- listen. . . properly, without doing ten other things at the same time (parents are very busy people!)
- focus on the way you play and whether you're having fun and improving as a footballer
- motivate you to work hard and put in effort.

Quote | The importance of not pressuring athletes to "win early" in their careers, but to teach values such as hard work, optimism and a "can do" attitude seem paramount. . . At the same time, parents emphasized the attitude "if you are going to do it, do it right". They also modelled a hard work ethic, held high (but reasonable) expectations and standards for their child and emphasized a "stick to it" attitude.'

Dan Gould, 'The development of psychological talent in US Olympic champions', 2002

Role models

So, do parents still have an effect on you as a player as you get older? Certainly, the role a parent plays in the early years will help to shape your interest and attitude. This is not just through supporting you, but also through watching football in a wider sense. Sitting together to watch a match on television or going to a match together helps forge a bond and gives an opportunity to share thoughts on the way the game is played. For example:

- How do you think Gerrard played today?
- Would you play Jones in that position?
- Have you seen how much space their midfield has been allowed?
- Do you think that was a fair tackle?

Informal chatting around questions like these helps you to gain a keen understanding of the way the game is played, the positions, the attitudes, the pace and the roles of the individual players within each team. This can all be related back to your own experience as a player, and will have an influence on the way you play.

All through your development as a player you have hopefully had the backing and support of your parents. It may be in a small way, such as making your drink or washing your kit, or in a much greater way such as managing your team. As you mature and develop as a player this role can be reversed, with you as a player giving your parents the opportunity to feel involved. After training, talk to them about the session. What did you learn? How did you feel? Was it an enjoyable session? Don't wait for questions; show them that you value their interest. After a match, talk about the way the game went, the highs and lows and, if they watched, ask them what they thought about the match. Try to be positive and you are likely to get a positive response.

Most importantly, you are the link between your coach and your parents. Any information given to you by your coach concerning dates of matches, kick-off times or changes to training needs to be passed on to your parents. It can be incredibly frustrating as a coach or manager if information isn't passed on and only six players turn up at a rearranged match. This works both ways – any messages from your parents, perhaps concerning holidays away, need to be passed on to your coach or manager.

Coaching principles

Football coaches come in many shapes, sizes and styles, but they all share one quality: a desire to improve their players and their team. Some have more success than others in achieving this! All coaches have beliefs and opinions about what coaching is and how coaches can help players. Many will have been playing football for more years than they care to mention, others will be huge football fans, with a fantastic knowledge about football. Some will be trained and qualified FA coaches, others will be willing volunteers with no qualifications but plenty of enthusiasm.

For all these types of coaches, much of their success or failure depends on their principles – their ethics, sense of fair play and their codes of behaviour. These have a direct impact on the players. You may have been a player in a number of teams, with a variety of different coaches and each will have developed their own style of coaching. Think about your coach, or a coach from a previous team, and consider these questions about their coaching principles:

- Does the coach shout from the touchline? Is it constructive?
- Are you encouraged to enjoy the game?
- Is winning all-important?
- Are players punished for a poor performance?
- What is the view of your coach on swearing?
- Does the coach communicate well with all the players?
- What is the view of your coach on cheating?
- Are you encouraged to accept refereeing decisions?
- Do all players have a chance to play?

The principles of your coach will affect the way you play the game. The principles a coach upholds will be evident in their behaviour towards others, and in how they expect you as a player to behave towards them. As well as playing as a footballer, you may want to coach a team in the future, so bear the following principles in mind.

Principles of successful coaching might include:
- respecting the needs of individuals and treating all players fairly
- developing independence by encouraging players and other coaches to accept responsibility for their own behaviour
- the development of individuals as people as well as football players
- the development of mutual trust, respect and commitment
- positive acknowledgement of progress and achievement
- communication with players, coaches, parents and other helpers
- promoting fair play within the laws of the game and respecting the dignity of opponents and officials

- accepting responsibility for the conduct of players and encouraging positive social and moral behaviours
- maintaining confidentiality of information when appropriate to do so
- displaying high personal standards of behaviour, dress and communication
- ensuring as far as possible the safety and health of players
- developing personal competence as a coach.

(Based on the FA Sport and Recreation 'Values Statement for Coaching, Teaching and Instructing', 2000)

Working with a coach

If you ask a coach what they value most in a player, many will state the ability to listen. Players are more likely to improve their skills and techniques by concentrating when they are asked to listen to any instructions. Any information or advice given is then internalized and can be transferred to the physical action. Obviously this can be a problem if the coach isn't particularly inspiring or if other players around have a poor attitude. However, this is an important life skill as it concerns a feeling of respect for others, and will say a lot about you as a person as well as a player. If you listen well, you are also likely to ask more questions, sharing the responsibility for improving yourself as a player and the team as a whole.

Talking to the coach, listening, asking questions. . . this is all about communication. It is a two-way process, and many players forget to respond positively to their coach. So be friendly and supportive, talk to the coach if things are going wrong or going well, and don't forget to thank your coach at the end of a training session or match.

Effort is another quality highly rated by coaches. If you work hard in training, try things out, and concentrate on improving your skills and technique, you will get more out of the training and are likely to increase your enjoyment. Show the same effort and commitment in matches and you will definitely be a valued team member, for the other players and the coach. This is particularly true if things aren't going well in a match. If winning and losing is all-important, with too much emphasis being placed on the result, it is very easy to 'give up' when being beaten. There is a sense of failure and some individuals are likely to withdraw their effort and behave in a negative way to 'protect' their own perceived ability at football.

These 'ego-oriented' individuals see success in terms of winning and out-performing others, with even greater success if they put in little effort to win. A 'task-oriented' player sees success in terms of getting better by trying harder. Research has shown that these players will remain motivated even when they are losing, because success is not based purely on the result, but on trying hard to improve. For example, a centre-forward who misses a few chances will continue to run into space in the attacking third of the field and accept the responsibility of taking shots at goal. If this is an 'ego-oriented' player, they are likely to put in less effort and drift further and further back after missing a few chances. Coaches find this behaviour difficult to understand, but it is often based on a player's early experiences of playing in a team. It is not too late to change, but you need to be aware of the differences. It is also worth pointing out that top professional footballers have a mixture of high-ego and high-task orientation – they have a strong desire to win and put in a huge amount of effort to improve as a player. What sort of player are you – ego-oriented or task-oriented?

Choosing a club

Finding a football club that is right for you can be a difficult decision and you are likely to need the support of your parents. The easiest option is to follow your friends to a particular club or to join your nearest one. Although this can often be the best reason for choosing a club, other factors should be considered. To begin with, think of the sort of football you want to play and ask yourself the following questions:

- **How much commitment do you want to give to training and matches?**
- **Are you able to play regularly on a Saturday or Sunday?**
- **How far are you willing to travel?**
- **What standard do you want to achieve?**
- **Do you want to play for a team that has a fun 'everyone plays' philosophy, or do you want a competitive environment (or a bit of both)?**

Once you've considered this, make a list of the clubs that are available to you:

- **Contact your local County Football Association or local organization. They will be able to provide you with a list of clubs and programmes being offered in your area.**
- **Ask friends and their parents and get their views.**
- **Ask at your school, as many clubs have developed excellent relationships with their local school.**
- **Look in the local press and on the Internet for contact details of clubs in your locality.**

Once you are ready to contact or visit a club, find out the background information on the club by checking its website, looking at any brochures or by talking to club officials. Consider the following:

- **Is the club FA affiliated and part of a local league organization?**
- **Has the club got 'Charter Standard' or 'Community Club' status?**

- How experienced and qualified are the coaches?
- Do they cater for a range of age groups for boys and girls?
- What are the facilities at the club like?
- Does the club have social and fund-raising events?
- What is the club's philosophy?
- What are the selection procedures? (For example, does missing training mean that a player is left out of the team?)
- Does the club have a code of conduct? (See pages 199–206.)
- Does the club follow the FA child protection procedures? (This should be a definite yes!)
- Who are the club officials – chair, secretary, treasurer etc?

In England the FA has a club recognition programme – Charter Standard Clubs. If a club you are looking at has this status, then that will certainly help answer a lot of the questions above. To receive the FA Charter Standard kitemark, clubs must demonstrate safe, quality practice. This includes:

- qualified coaches
- child protection trained staff and policy
- codes of conduct
- fair play.

The next step is to visit the club. Here are a few tips on what to look out for on your first visit, perhaps to watch training or a match:

- Is there a welcoming atmosphere?
- Do the players look like they are enjoying the football?
- Are there parents watching or do they keep away?
- What is the relationship like between the coach and the players?

- **Is there a good coach to player ratio?** Generally, this should be two coaches per squad, with a maximum 1:16 ratio.

Once you are a member of a team, try to get involved with the club in a broader way. Go along to any social events and support them in fund-raising activities. If they need volunteer help in, say, running a mini-soccer event, put your name forward. The more you get involved, the more you will get out of being part of the club.

Becoming a coach

Some of you may have a desire to continue your interest in football beyond just playing the game. Coaching football is a tremendous way to give back to grassroots players some of the skills and attributes that you have developed over the years. Once you make a start on the coaching journey you will become a valued member of the community and, for some of you, it may even influence the path your career takes.

As soon as you reach the age of 16, you are able to start your coaching development by taking the FA's level 1 coaching award. Although you may feel you have a good understanding of the game, the course looks at much more than just training drills and tactics and is a valuable exercise for anyone looking to play a role in coaching. It is also the first rung on the ladder and an important one for providing you with the FA philosophy for coaches.

For those interested in coaching, Table 10.1 shows the development of courses and awards for coaches in England.

Table 10.1 **Courses and awards for coaches in England**

Course	For Whom	Prerequisites	Where
Coaching Level 1	Coaches of young players.	Open entry course for anybody aged over 16 years of age. You don't need any experience, just an interest in the game and motivation to improve your knowledge.	Locally run courses managed by County FA's as well as residentially run courses at approved FA centres.
Coaching Level 2	Coaches with some experience at any level with regular participation.	Open entry course for anybody aged over 16 years of age with regular practical experience of participation of football.	Locally run courses managed by County FA's as well as residentially run courses at approved FA centres.
Coaching Level 3 /UEFA 'B'	Coaches that are working with a team over an extensive period.	Anybody over 18 years of age. Candidates must hold the Level 2 Coaching Certificate.	Locally run courses managed by County FA's as well as residentially run courses at approved FA centres.
UEFA 'A'	Coaches with experience at representative level.	Candidates must hold the Level 3 /UEFA 'B' Certificate in Coaching.	Nationally run course that takes place residentially at approved FA centres.

For more information and to enrol on a course visit www.TheFA.com/FALearning

Codes of conduct

The FA expects certain standards from all those involved in the game, whether players, officials, parents or coaches, at whatever level of play. A set of guidelines for clubs has been issued, which outlines the standards expected from the FA. This is set out below.

FA Code of Conduct for football

1 General

Football is the national game. All those involved with the game at every level and whether as a player, match official, coach or administrator, have a responsibility, above and beyond compliance with the law, to act according to the highest standards of integrity, and to ensure that the reputation of the game is, and remains high. This code applies to all those involved in football under the auspices of the Football Association.

2 Community

Football at all levels is a vital part of a community. Football will take into account community feelings when making decisions.

3 Equality

Football is opposed to discrimination of any form and will promote measures to prevent it, in whatever form, from being expressed.

4 Participants

Football recognizes the sense of ownership felt by those who participate at all levels of the game. This includes those who play, those who coach or help in any way, and those who officiate, as well as administrators and supporters. Football is committed to appropriate consultation.

5 Young people

Football acknowledges the extent of its influence over young people and pledges to set a positive example.

6 Propriety

Football acknowledges that public confidence demands the highest standards of financial and administrative behaviour within the game, and will not tolerate corruption or improper practices.

7 Trust and respect

Football will uphold a relationship of trust and respect between all involved in the game, whether they are individuals, clubs or other organizations.

8 Violence

Football rejects the use of violence of any nature by anyone involved in the game.

9 Fairness

Football is committed to fairness in its dealings with all involved in the game.

10 Integrity and fair play

Football is committed to the principle of playing to win consistent with fair play.

FA Code of Conduct for coaches

1 Coaches are the key to the establishment of ethics in football. The concept of ethics and their attitude directly affects the behaviour of players under their supervision. Coaches are, therefore, expected to pay particular attention to the moral aspects of their conduct. Coaches have to be aware that almost all of their everyday decisions and choices, as well as strategic targets, have ethical implications.

2 It is natural that winning constitutes a basic concern for coaches. This code is not intended to conflict with that. However, the code calls for coaches to disassociate themselves from a 'win at all costs' attitude.

3 Increased responsibility is requested from coaches involved in coaching young people. The health, safety, welfare and moral

education of young people are a first priority, before the achievement or the reputation of the club, coach or parent.

4 Set out below is the FA Coaches Association Code of Conduct (which reflects the standards expressed by the National Coaching Foundation and the National Association of Sports Coaches) which forms the benchmark for all involved in coaching:

a Coaches must respect the rights, dignity and worth of each and every person and treat each equally within the context of the sport.

b Coaches must place the well-being and safety of each player above all other considerations, including the development of performance.

c Coaches must adhere to all guidelines laid down by governing bodies.

d Coaches must develop an appropriate working relationship with each player based on mutual trust and respect.

e Coaches must not exert undue influence to obtain personal benefit or reward.

f Coaches must encourage and guide players to accept responsibility for their own behaviour and performance.

g Coaches must ensure that the activities they direct or advocate are appropriate for the age, maturity, experience and ability of players.

h Coaches should, at the outset, clarify with the players (and, where appropriate, parents) exactly what is expected of them and also what they are entitled to expect from their coach.

i Coaches must cooperate fully with other specialists (e.g. other coaches, officials, sports scientists, doctors, and physiotherapists) in the best interests of the players.

j Coaches must always promote the positive aspects of the sport (e.g. fair play) and never condone violations of the laws of the game, behaviour contrary to the spirit of the laws of the game or relevant rules and regulations or the use of prohibited substances or techniques.

k   Coaches must consistently display high standards of behaviour and appearance.

l   Coaches must not use or tolerate inappropriate language.

FA Code of Conduct for players

1   Players are the most important people in the sport. Playing for the team, and for the team to win, is the most fundamental part of the game. But not winning at any cost – fair play and respect for others is of utmost importance.

2   This code is derived from one that focuses on players involved in top-class football. Nevertheless, the key concepts in the code are valid for players at all levels.

a   Obligations towards the game

A player should:

- Make every effort to develop their own sporting abilities, in terms of skill, technique, tactics and stamina.

- Give maximum effort and strive for the best possible performance during a game, even if his team is in a position where the desired result has already been achieved.

- Set a positive example to others, particularly young players and supporters.

- Avoid all forms of gamesmanship and time wasting.

- Always have regard for the best interests of the game, including where publicly expressing an opinion on the game and any particular aspect of it, including others involved in the game.

- Not use inappropriate language.

b   Obligations towards one's own team

A player should:

- Make every effort consistent with fair play and the laws of the game to help his own team win.

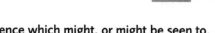

- Resist any influence which might, or might be seen to, bring into question his commitment to the team winning.

c Respect for the laws of the game and competition rules

A player should:

- Know and abide by the laws, rules and spirit of the game, and the competition rules.

- Accept success and failure, victory and defeat, equally.

- Resist any temptation to take banned substances or use banned techniques.

d Respect towards opponents

A player should:

- Treat opponents with due respect at all times, irrespective of the result of the game.

- Safeguard the physical fitness of opponents, avoid violence and rough play, and help injured opponents.

e Respect towards match officials

A player should:

- Accept the decisions of the match officials without protest.

- Avoid words or actions that may mislead match officials.

- Show due respect towards match officials.

f Respect towards team officials

A player should:

- Abide by the instructions of their coach and team officials, provided they do not contradict the spirit of the code.

- Show due respect towards the team officials of the opposition.

g Obligations towards the supporters

A player should:

- Show due respect to the interests of supporters.

FA Code of Conduct for team officials

This code applies to all team/club officials (although some elements may not apply to all officials).

1 Obligations towards the game

The team official should:

- Set a positive example for others, particularly young players and supporters.
- Promote and develop his own team, having regard to the interests of the players, supporters and the reputation of the national game.
- Share knowledge and experience when invited to do so, taking into account the interest of the body that has requested this rather than personal interests.
- Avoid all forms of gamesmanship.
- Show due respect to match officials and others involved in the game.
- Always have regard for the best interests of the game, including where publicly expressing an opinion of the game and any particular aspect of it, including others involved in the game.
- Not use or tolerate inappropriate language.

2 Obligations towards the team

The team official should:

- Make every effort to develop the sporting, technical and tactical levels of the club/team, and to obtain the best results for the team, using all permitted means.
- Give priority to the interests of the team over individual interests.
- Resist all illegal or unsporting influences, including banned substances and techniques.
- Promote ethical principles.
- Show due respect for the interests of the players, coaches and officials, their own club/team and others.

3 **Obligations towards supporters**

The team official should:

• Show due respect for the interests of supporters.

4 **Respect towards match officials**

The team official should:

• Accept the decisions of the match officials without protest.

• Avoid words or actions that may mislead a match official.

• Show due respect towards match officials.

FA Code of Conduct for parents/spectators

1 Parents/spectators have a great influence on children's enjoyment and success in football. All children play football because they first and foremost love the game – it's fun. Remember that however good a child becomes at football within the club it is important to reinforce the message to parents/spectators that positive encouragement will contribute to:

• children enjoying football

• a sense of personal achievement

• self-esteem

• improving the child's skills and techniques.

2 A parent's/spectator's expectations and attitudes have a significant bearing on a child's attitude towards:

• Other players.

• Officials.

• Managers.

• Spectators.

3 Parents/spectators will be positive and encouraging towards all children, not just their own.

4 Parents/spectators are encouraged to:

• Applaud the opposition as well as our own teams.

• Avoid coaching during the game.

- refrain from shouting and screaming
- respect the referee's decisions
- give attention to each of the children involved in football, not just the most talented
- give encouragement to everyone to participate in football.

5 Parents and spectators should be made aware of these issues together with the club's other adopted codes of conduct and child protection policy.

Summary

- **Your parents or carers will have a major impact on your desire, attitudes, values and ambitions.**

- **Most parents start off with good intentions and may need your support to remain positive.**

- **Much of the success or failure of a coach depends on their principles – their ethics, sense of fair play and codes of behaviour.**

- **Effort and good communication from players are highly-valued by coaches.**

- **If you are in a position where you need to choose a club, put some time and research into choosing one that is right for you.**

Self testers

1 Think of three ways to involve your parents positively in your interest in football.

2 Describe some of the principles of successful coaching. Give four examples.

3 What are the requirements for a club to achieve Charter Standard in England?

Action plan

Consider your attitudes and behaviour during training sessions and matches. For the next four matches and training sessions, make a conscious effort to listen carefully, communicate more and put in more effort. Monitor the difference this makes to you as a player.

References

Motivation: More than a Question of Winning and Losing (1999), Darren C. Treasure, Assistant Professor of Sport and Exercise Psychology, Arizona State University

Chapter 11

Evaluating your performance

THIS CHAPTER WILL:
- Explain how a goal-setting programme can improve your game.
- Show the three stages for implementing a goal-setting programme.
- Give a practical example of a weekly goal-setting diary.

Why set goals?

Sport psychologists have identified goal-setting as an effective way to help players prepare for competition and improve technical, physical and mental performance. It involves the establishment of specific targets that show what a player, with or without the involvement of a coach, is striving to achieve.

Goal-setting should be seen as a method of helping you to develop your areas of weakness and maintain your strengths. This chapter focuses specifically on the development of the individual rather than the team.

Types of goal

Training goals

Training goals can improve performance by directing attention towards specific aspects of personal development as well as by generating the effort needed to make progress. Training goals are often organized through a framework that features long- and short-term goals (see below).

Competition goals

'Process' goals can be used to influence the way you approach games. They can focus on specific tasks before a match, such as closing down quickly or being aware of movement off the ball. It is important to focus your attention on the process rather than the outcome of the match.

Long-term goals

These identify what a player or coach wants to achieve. They are usually stated in general terms and reflect a player's aspirations and ambitions. An example could be for a player to establish themselves as a 'regular' in his/her local team, or to successfully recover from an injury.

Short-term goals

These are more precise and associated with daily/weekly 'action steps'. Short-term goals and 'action steps' can influence what takes place at your team's training session or they may relate to your individual practice time. Short-term goals relate to practical action which can lead to achieving your long-term goals. An example may be to improve short passing skills.

Statistics

Goal-setting and targets are used by professional football clubs to help the development of the players at their academies and centres of excellence.

It may be better understood if players think of the short-term and long-term goals being linked as a staircase (see Figure 11.1). At the top of the staircase is the long-term goal, with the short-term goals being represented by the progression of stairs. Achieving short-term goals improves the likelihood that long-term goals will be reached.

Figure 11.1 **An example of a goal-setting staircase**

> **Establish myself as a 'regular' player in my local team.**
>
> Maintain concentration for the full game.
>
> Improve fitness level.
>
> Improve accuracy of passing.
>
> Improve communication on the pitch.
>
> Improve ball control.

In simple terms:

commitment to action steps = short-term goals achieved = long-term goals realized

---

Top tip

Be realistic! You need to be realistic about the amount of time and effort you can put into a goal-setting programme.

The three stages for implementing a goal-setting programme

Before setting a programme, it is important that you spend some time evaluating your game – your strengths, weaknesses and long-term goals. You can do this on your own or, even better, by involving a supportive parent or coach. The coach or parent can oversee the programme and alter and develop it over time. Table 11.1 sets out the three stages involved in a goal-setting programme.

Table 11.1 **Goal-setting stages**

Stage 1	Stage 2	Stage 3
Establish the way forward	*Set goals*	*Monitor, maintain and evaluate*
Meeting/discussion.	Goal-setting programme should come from the meeting/discussion.	Formal or informal meetings to reflect on progress and consider any changes.
Consider your strengths and weaknesses.	Establish long-terms goals.	Whenever possible, record progress in writing.
The coach, if involved, should become familiar with your views about your own ability as well as any personal targets.	Identify short-term goals (what has to be done to achieve the long-term goals).	Check the time you have given and how long it is taking to achieve short- and long-term goals.
Coach should share his/her views on how you could improve.	Make sure the goals are: **S**pecific **M**easurable **A**chievable/adjustable **R**ealistic/recorded **T**ime phased.	This stage allows for new challenges and targets to be set.

Quote

'I love seeing players improve when you work on technique. You need different programmes for different-sized goalies. They're not all 6ft 5in. The big ones need sharpness, mobility. The smaller ones need spring and to learn how to give themselves presence.'

Alan Hodgkinson, Oxford Utd goalkeeping coach and former England goalkeeper.

Alan 'discovered' Peter Schmeichel and David Seaman

Top tip

Make sure that when you set a goal programme, the goals are SMART.

Keeping a goal-setting diary

It is a good idea to keep a weekly goal-setting diary. Over the page is an example of one that has been completed. Use this model to start your own diary.

WEEKLY GOAL-SETTING DIARY　　DATE:

Short-term goal for this week:
Develop my sideways
diving technique

Action steps	**Thoughts**

Monday

*Work with team-mate/coach
on low diving to either side.
Think about set position to
start from.*

*Stronger on left side than
right – take extra step
forward to spring off.
Work on catching the ball
rather than parrying it.*

Tuesday
No training.

Wednesday

*Five-a-side match with
team-mates.
Goal – I will focus on diving
technique as well as other
basic skills.*

*Some good diving saves –
comments from other players!
I enjoyed the match and was
pleased with my performance..*

Thursday

*Team training session
Coach to organize high
and low diving drills.
Goal – in drills I will focus
on landing position and
catching the ball.*

*My sideways diving to either
side has improved. I am
starting to feel more
confident.*

Friday

*School match.
Goal – think about good
set position so alert for
all attacks.*

*Satisfied with my performance
as catching and diving
technique has improved
though coach felt I could be
more dominant in the box
for crosses.*

Summary

- **Goal-setting can help you to organize your training and ensure that important areas of development have a focus.**

- **It is important to establish long- and short-term goals for training and to use process type goals as part of your preparation for playing competitive football.**

- **Goal-setting should be written down and reviewed on a regular basis.**

- **The more effort you put into your goal-setting programme the greater the chance of success in improving your play.**

Self-tester

- What are the three key stages in a goal-setting programme?
- Describe action steps.
- What does SMART stand for?

Action plan

Consider developing your own goal-setting programme using the three-stage approach covered in this chapter. Start by planning a diary and arranging a meeting with your coach.

You may find *The Official FA Guide to Psychology for Football* by Dr Andy Cale useful.

Index

Master the Game
Defender

Achieve your potential

Master the Game: Defender gives you the skills and essential advice you need to perfect this key position. It helps you master the specific skills and techniques that are fundamental to becoming a great defender, and covers nutritional, fitness and psychological aspects of player performance.

This book enables you to:
- **understand the key principles of play**
- **prepare for the game**
- **improve your skills, from heading to tough tackling**
- **learn from your match performance.**

Packed full of indispensable tips and techniques, this book will soon enhance your ability and increase your enjoyment of the world's greatest game.

Paul Broadbent is the manager and coach of an under-16s football team and a widely published author. **Andrew Allen** is a development manager for school sport and an FA qualified coach.

Master the Game
Midfielder

Achieve your potential

Master the Game: Midfielder gives you the skills and essential advice
you need to perfect this key position. It helps you master the specific
skills and techniques that are fundamental to becoming a great
midfielder, and covers nutritional, fitness and psychological aspects of
player performance.

This book enables you to:
- **understand the key principles of play**
- **prepare for the game**
- **improve your skills, from ball control to passing**
- **learn from your match performance.**

Packed full of indispensable tips and techniques, this book will soon
enhance your ability and increase your enjoyment of the world's
greatest game.

Paul Broadbent is the manager and coach of an under-16s
football team and a widely published author. **Andrew Allen** is a
development manager for school sport and an FA qualified coach.

Master the Game
Striker

Achieve your potential

Master the Game: Striker gives you the skills and essential advice you need to perfect this key position. It helps you master the specific skills and techniques that are fundamental to becoming a great striker, and covers nutritional, fitness and psychological aspects of player performance.

This book enables you to:
- **understand the key principles of play**
- **prepare for the game**
- **improve your skills, from sharp shooting to agility**
- **learn from your match performance.**

Packed full of indispensable tips and techniques, this book will soon enhance your ability and increase your enjoyment of the world's greatest game.

Paul Broadbent is the manager and coach of an under-16s football team and a widely published author. **Andrew Allen** is a development manager for school sport and an FA qualified coach.

THE OFFICIAL FA GUIDE TO
FITNESS FOR FOOTBALL

Be a part of the game

The Official FA Guide to Fitness for Football provides essential knowledge and advice for everyone who plays the game.

This book includes:
- **basic physiology and nutrition**
- **training strategies**
- **the physiological differences between adults and children.**

Packed with practical exercises, information and expert advice, this book will improve your understanding and enhance your ability and enjoyment of the world's greatest game.

The author, **Dr Richard Hawkins**, is the Deputy Head of Exercise Science at The Football Association.

FA Learning
'learning through football'

TheFA.com/FALearning

Visit the website for information on all FA Learning's educational activities.

The FA

LEARNING

THE OFFICIAL FA GUIDE TO
BASIC TEAM COACHING

Be a part of the game

The Official FA Guide to Basic Team Coaching covers all the
essential aspects of coaching and is vital for those who coach
amateur football, or who are considering becoming a coach.

This book includes:
- **team strategies and tactics**
- **leadership and management**
- **match analysis.**

Packed with practical exercises, information and expert advice,
this book will improve your understanding and enhance your
ability and enjoyment of the world's greatest game.

The author, **Les Reed**, is The FA's Acting Technical Director and
was formerly the Assistant Manager at Charlton Athletic. Les has
coached England players at every level from youth to senior teams.

FA Learning
'learning through football'

TheFA.com/FALearning

Visit the website for information on all FA
Learning's educational activities.

THE OFFICIAL FA GUIDE TO
PSYCHOLOGY FOR FOOTBALL

Be a part of the game

The Official FA Guide to Psychology for Football is an introductory guide for anyone who wants to understand the needs of young players.

This book includes:
- **understanding the motivation, learning and development of players**
- **the affect of a player's environment**
- **how to develop individual strategies.**

Packed with practical exercises, information and expert advice, this book will improve your understanding and enhance your ability and enjoyment of the world's greatest game.

The author, **Dr Andy Cale**, is The Football Association's Education Advisor and was previously a lecturer in Sports Psychology at Loughborough University.

FA Learning
'learning through football'

TheFA.com/FALearning

Visit the website for information on all FA Learning's educational activities.

LEARNING

THE OFFICIAL FA GUIDE:
A PARENT'S GUIDE TO FOOTBALL

Be a part of the game

The Official FA Guide: A Parent's Guide to Football is essential reading for any parent of a young footballer, who wants to get involved and help their child to do their very best.

This book includes:
- **choosing a club and being involved in it**
- **sharing the football interest**
- **being a 'garden coach'.**

Packed with practical exercises, information and expert advice, this book will improve your understanding and enhance your ability and enjoyment of the world's greatest game.

The author, **Les Howie**, is responsible for the development of all clubs in the non-professional national game for The Football Association.

FA Learning
'learning through football'

TheFA.com/FALearning

Visit the website for information on all FA Learning's educational activities.